# Revenge is Sweet

# Revenge is Sweet

### Settling Scores,
### Getting Even
### and
### Other Ingenious Stories
### of Retribution

### Claire Gillman

First published in 2006 by Fusion Press,
a division of Satin Publications Ltd
101 Southwark Street
London SE1 0JF
UK
info@visionpaperbacks.co.uk
www.visionpaperbacks.co.uk
Publisher: Sheena Dewan

ISBN-13: 978-1-905745-01-2
ISBN-10: 1-905745-01-x

2 4 6 8 10 9 7 5 3 1

Cover and text design by ok?design
Printed and bound in the UK by Cox and Wyman Ltd,
Reading, Berkshire

# Contents

# Introduction

*'Don't get mad, get even.'*
*Robert F Kennedy,*
*US Attorney General, Senator (1925–1968)*

How many times have you blasted your horn at another inconsiderate driver and then spent the rest of your journey plotting what you should have done to the other motorist to ruin his day in return? Have you ever wanted to 'pay some-one back' after a hurtful comment or argument, or wished to 'settle the score' after a friend or loved one breaks your trust or betrays your confidence?

I bet there are not many of you who are blameless. Can you hand on heart tell me that you have never harboured thoughts of getting even with someone who has done you wrong? Never wanted to teach some miscreant a lesson?

The truth is that in response to a real or perceived hurt or slight, the vast majority of people want to retaliate. Most do it in thought alone – but a few retaliate in deed, wreaking revenge on the original transgressor either physically or through a carefully hatched plan.

In this book, I have sought to find some humorous tales of when people all around the world seek to settle the score. It takes a light-hearted look at the darker side of human nature and stories have been gathered from the far-flung corners of the earth. In fact, every single inhabited continent is represented in our catalogue of revenge stories.

And that's because the desire for revenge is common to us all, regardless of creed, colour, gender or race. Interestingly though, those bent on revenge tend to favour a certain approach depending on where they were brought up and, to some extent, whether they are male or female. But before you flick to chapters two and three to decide for yourselves which sex is the most vengeful, let's briefly take a look at what prompts all of us to want revenge in the first place.

## Why do we want revenge?

Apart from the obvious answer, namely that it makes us feel better, the psychologists will tell you that we are acting in response to our emotions when it comes to seeking revenge and that the primary motivation in seeking retribution is either anger or fear.

If you take the scenario of some lunatic on the road cutting you up, you can see how anger is a prime motivation in wanting to get even with said road hog. You pump the horn, you shout and gesticulate – yes, you're pretty angry. You can accept that. But fear? Not immediately obvious in that scenario is it, except if you consider that all of us, but men in particular, have a fear of losing face. If you let the driver who pushes in front of you in the queue of traffic do so without some sign of resistance or desire for retribution, will you be seen – or worse still, perceive yourself – as feeble or a pushover in some way?

It's small wonder that we're confused on the subject of revenge. Most of us know that it is petty-minded or mean-spirited to want revenge, but we also know how satisfying it would be to even the score. This confusion comes in part from the mixed messages we received from our parents. On the one hand, we were told not to retaliate, particularly against siblings: 'Let Mummy and Daddy sort it out,' they would say (as you set fire to your brother's homework because he'd cut your doll's hair). On the other hand, our parents would exhort us to stand up for ourselves: 'Don't let the big kids push you around. Teach him a lesson.' A mixed message, if ever there was one. Little boys in particular grow up believing that to be a real man, you have to stick up for yourself. Don't start the aggression, but finish it.

Quite apart from childhood conditioning, the cards are stacked more heavily in favour of us choosing revenge over 'turning the other cheek' than you might at first think.

It appears that, in psychological terms, forgiveness is not something that comes naturally to humans. In a research paper by Sells and Hargrave in 1998, they describe forgiveness as 'the antithesis of the individual's natural and predictable response to violation and victimisation'.

Our natural desire for justice means that we want to get even because that's only fair – it restores the natural order of things. In particular, if no law has been broken and a wronged person cannot expect justice through official channels, then he or she may well be tempted to take the law into their own hands.

A Canadian research project into revenge led by Assistant Professor of Psychology, Stacey L Nairn PhD of the University of Prince Edward Island, reveals that extracting 'an eye for an eye', which basically means you do to the original transgressor no more and no less than they did to you, is generally considered acceptable and much better than 'turning the other cheek' or going too far.

Professor Nairn says, 'My findings do suggest that although we've all been taught to turn the other cheek in the face of transgressions, particularly mild ones such as the one used in our study, apparently the lesson hasn't sunken in. Restoration of justice or balance seems to be more important in people's deliberations concerning the type of response that is most appropriate in the face of transgressions.'

## Vengeful Women and Merciless Men

To date, all the scientific research has shown that men are more likely to engage in acts of revenge than women and that the degree of retaliation is likely to be more serious when men are involved than women.

I have to say, though, that when looking for the stories for this book I have found the opposite is true. For every revenge story that I found perpetrated by a man, there were ten stories concerning a woman. In truth, the vast majority of these stories tended to be regarding matters of the heart, which probably supports the age-old adage about 'hell hath no fury like a woman scorned'. But perhaps the experts are right, and it is just that women like to recount their revenge experiences more than men.

Baffled by the conflicting findings, I decided to conduct a small semi-scientific research project of my own. Well, actually I asked a group of ten friends over a few drinks whether any of them had committed acts of revenge. Of the five men and five women present, three of the men spoke in loose terms about a 'mate' who'd wreaked vengeance, and all confessed to some pretty rash and spiteful driving stunts in order to wipe the smile off another motorist's face (naturally, the original crime had been forgotten in the heat of getting even). Conversely, the women were keeping pretty tight-lipped on the subject, although one confessed later in private that she had carried out a heinous act of revenge (involving private parts and chilli powder!) on an old boyfriend who'd dumped her, but she hadn't wanted to confess in front of her husband. So, it seems, both theories hold water. My quick straw poll shows that the boffins are right – men do appear to seek revenge more often than women, but there's more than a grain of truth in my original findings too. Women are just as capable of revenge but generally limit acts of vengeance to affairs of the heart.

But, enough of my amateur sleuthing. Let's get back to some more juicy facts, such as the recent Canadian research that shows that, depending on whether the original transgressor and the person seeking revenge is a man or a woman, it affects how we feel about the vengeful acts.

Men view women who seek revenge on a male transgressor more negatively than when a man gets his own back on either a man or woman who instigated events, whereas women don't take the sex of those involved into account at all (Nairn *et al*, 2006).

The Canadian research project centred on revenge involving male/female friendships and the findings supported previous studies (Bem, 1981 and Baumeister, 2004) where men adhered to gender stereotypes, namely that a 'real man' should never hit a woman and 'nice girls' don't get even. No wonder men get such a surprise when they trade the wife in for a younger model and the ex cuts up nasty – they just don't think we women have it in us. Not surprisingly, just as in the more recent study, the women in these trials were not influenced at all by gender stereotypes.

However, if you raise the stakes, research carried out in 2005 (Forbes *et al*) into revenge after a serious sexual betrayal in a romantic relationship (as opposed to casual friendships) showed somewhat different results. They found that although generally hitting and getting even were considered unjustified, if a betrayed woman hits a man that is more justified than if a betrayed man hits his female partner.

When you consider it, none of us wince too much if the movies show a woman slapping the face of her cheating lover but we're all horrified if the man does the same. But, I think we'd all agree that Glenn Close has gone a wee step too far when she resorts to boiling the family bunny and rearing out of a bath full of water clutching a bread knife intent on murder after Michael Douglas rejects her romantic attentions in *Fatal Attraction*.

Another research project, from Florida University, takes the subject of revenge within relationships one step further. They presented a large sample of men and women with scenarios in which a partner was sexually or emotionally unfaithful. The results will probably come as little surprise. Basically, men became more jealous in response to a perceived threat to their self-esteem, while women were more concerned with infidelity that threatened their relationship.

Or, in other words, men are more likely than women to become jealous over sexual infidelity, and women over emotional infidelity.

## Revenge throughout History

There is practically no society today that does not have a history of blood revenge somewhere in its past. Before the emergence of central government and their legal and judicial systems, the main source of authority came from family and kinship ties. As a result, an entire family was considered responsible for whatever one of them had done and for avenging transgressions against members of the family.

This became known as blood revenge or blood feuds and this cycle of retaliatory violence, with the relatives of someone who has been killed or wronged seeking vengeance by killing or otherwise physically punishing the culprits and/ or their relatives, was widespread.

In Celtic society, for example, disputes and insults between families and clans demanded 'an eye for an eye' and often ended in murder. In the same way, retribution would be sought in response to raids for cattle, valuables or slaves from neighbouring tribes. These blood feuds and actions were carried on for generations in Celtic strongholds such as Scotland, Ireland and Appalachia.

The same traditions can be seen in peoples ranging from Arabic countries to the Far East. In Japan's feudal past, it was the Samurai who enforced the law. They were duty-bound to uphold the honour of their family, clan or lord and would use revenge killings (*katakiuchi*) to this end (see Chapter 9, Military Revenge). Anyone who has seen Tarantino's *Kill Bill* movies, which borrowed heavily from Japanese martial arts and Samurai films, will know what I mean.

## Blood Money

**In the past, some wily citizens realised that blood feuds were getting out of hand and that there could be no end to the cycle of retaliation and violence. So, they devised something called blood money where a family would pay a certain amount to compensate the next of kin of a murder victim (accidental or intentional) and so terminate the feud.**

**This concept was used in Viking, Norse and Anglo-Saxon societies where it was known as *weregild* (literally translated meaning 'man money'). It was also referred to in Celtic culture as *ericfine*.**

**Although its use has pretty much universally died out, in certain Arab and Islamic countries, including Saudi Arabia, Iran and Pakistan, this tradition persists and has even found its way into legislation. There is a**

**tariff of defined rates for the lives of those killed, with bereaved families of a Muslim man receiving most and those of a Hindu woman receiving least. The rate for female victims is roughly half that for male victims.**

## Different Countries, Different Attitudes

In most parts of the developed world, central governments have taken over the responsibility of mediating in feuds and disputes, using police forces and the legal system.

However, in certain societies, people do not accept or respect the local law enforcement authority and prefer instead to settle their own scores.

Despite efforts to stamp this out, in areas such as Corsica, southern Italy (especially Sardinia, Sicily and Calabria), Crete and other areas of Greece, eastern regions of Turkey, Albania and India, vendettas, blood feuds and honour revenge attacks continue – sometimes in the full knowledge of the local police who turn a blind eye.

Similarly, in certain conservative sections of Muslim society, honour killings are still carried out, most frequently against a female member of a family who is believed to have transgressed the moral or sexual code of conduct.

Yet, even the law can take the desire for revenge into account in some modern societies. For example, in France *crime passionnel* (a crime of passion) is a valid defence during a murder case. So if a French husband catches his wife with her lover, flies into a rage and stabs them both to death, he could claim *crime passionnel* and possibly get away with it.

Certainly, in 1952, when Yvonne Chevallier shot her husband five times after he rejected her and publicly humiliated her with an open affair, the penal system allowed for a love-triangle provision (a vestige of the Napoleonic era), which absolved from punishment any man who committed homicide after finding his wife in bed with another man. The tables were turned and the law that was designed to protect men was invoked to assure Yvonne's freedom – apparently to the great delight of the French public.

## Turning the Other Cheek

Yet, despite all this, psychologists, doctors, politicians and spiritual leaders alike are all agreed that revenge and retaliation do not pay. We're told that by far the best course of action when you are wronged or attacked is to assume moral superiority and ignore the urge for vengeance. Dr Geoff Scobie, a psychologist at the University of Glasgow, terms this response 'compensation'. It makes those who have hurt you feel ashamed to have done so – simply because you have the moral high ground.

Hard though it may be, maintaining dignity and decorum, getting on with your life and living well, actually works. Seeking revenge can make you feel bad about yourself and, in some cases, simply flatter your oppressor. When you seek revenge, you are showing your tormentor that you are hurting.

Apparently, rather than seeking revenge, talking with those you trust and love about your predicament and the thoughts of revenge that you harbour is a better idea. Yes, it seems it's OK to fantasise about shaming your unfaithful girlfriend in front of her work colleagues or leaving your love-rat boyfriend's car on bricks, but you shouldn't go through with your plan.

In fact, the Canadian study supports the notion that if your partner has run off with someone else, telling friends and discussing what you'd like to do to the villain is beneficial and likely to reduce the chances of you taking action. Professor Nairn explains: 'My pilot study demonstrates that individuals' desire for revenge did indeed decrease after group discussion, as leniency shift would predict.' Talk it over with your friends or read a good book full of inspirational stories of revenge to fuel your daydreams(!) – that seems to be what the experts are saying.

Meanwhile, there is no harm in making sure that word gets back to the love-rat that you are not only getting on with your life, but living well without him/her. After all, people generally know when they have behaved badly. Living with the guilt should be punishment enough for them, particularly if you are putting salt in the wound by getting over it and living *la vida loca*.

## He Who Laughs Last Laughs Longest

But let's face it, not all of us are capable of such saintly behaviour. Even though we know that 'taking the moral high ground' works, turning your back on the chance of evening the score takes a lot of fortitude. If you're not the sort of person who is made of such stern stuff, then the experts recommend waiting before retaliating. According to a 1988 study, you are less likely to want revenge, if at all, if you give yourself time to deliberate.

So, while you're cooling your heels and calming your nerves, why not take a browse through the following pages that are packed full of amazing and funny stories of those who could not resist the urge for revenge? These tales have been harvested from personal accounts, the radio, television, newspapers, books and the internet. To warrant inclusion, the vast majority had to make me laugh. However, there are some revenge stories that have been included because they are ingenious and others that were just too amazing and outrageous to leave out.

I hope you enjoy the innovative, witty and wacky ways that people have chosen to gain their revenge and are

amused by the mishaps and calamities that befall both victims and perpetrators of our revenge stories. And, if you are
still craving vengeance at the end of this book, then at least
some of the stories you have read may prove inspirational
– and perhaps you can share your own tale of vengeance
with us for next time.

# Chapter One
# Female Revenge

*'Sweet is revenge – especially to women.'*
Don Juan, *Lord Byron (1788–1824)*

If you check out the numerous media stories that recount acts of revenge, the overwhelming message that shines through is that women have a strong and inflamed sense of injustice, particularly where their love life is concerned.

In fact, there are websites exclusively dedicated to women who want to 'name and shame' ex-partners who have done the dirty on them.

Take, for example, the American website dontdate-himgirl.com which describes itself as a 'search engine for cheating men'. If your man has cheated on you, this site offers you the chance to warn other women so they don't make the same mistake. You can even post a picture of the scoundrel.

## Revenge is Sweet

But rather than taking a position of moral superiority and claiming that their actions are to protect other women, most of the women in the revenge stories I've heard confess that basically they want to get even without getting into trouble.

Of course, the most infamous story of a woman seeking revenge on a physically abusive husband was that of Lorena Bobbitt who in 1993 cut off her husband John's penis with a kitchen knife while he slept. She then drove off in the car and threw the severed penis out of the window on the freeway. The Virginia police painstakingly searched the area and miraculously, found the severed appendage. Even more remarkably, surgeons managed to surgically reattach the penis.

When asked about her motives, Lorena explained that she was getting her own back for past abuses and because her husband was 'selfish' and 'wouldn't give her an orgasm'. She was found not guilty of 'malicious wounding' on grounds of temporary insanity and because of her husband's history of physical abuse.

Not surprisingly the couple divorced in 1995, but the incident has remained in popular culture around the world. In the States, it has been referred to in the lyrics of pop songs and in several films, including the 1999 movie, *Fight Club*, starring Brad Pitt. In the UK, 'doing a Bobbitt' entered the language as a threat used against the unwary husband!

None of the following stories are as extreme as the revenge that Lorena exacted on John Wayne Bobbit, but there are some remarkable examples of women wreaking vengeance and, in many cases, getting away with it. So, read on.

# Jilted and Dangerous

Women were once labelled the 'fairer' or 'gentler' sex but when you cast an eye over the following stories of devious and downright dastardly revenge – and bearing in mind the salutary tale of the 'Bobbitt' case – perhaps men should think twice about underestimating the gift for vengeance that a rejected woman possesses.

## Two Pints Today, Please

In 1992, Lady Graham-Moon struck a chord with women across Britain when she spectacularly and very publicly repaid her husband's infidelity with a destructive spree.

When, after 27 years, her second marriage to Sir Peter Graham-Moon ran out of steam, Lady Graham-Moon wanted it to end in a civilised manner. They both led separate lives while living in the same house, waiting for their decree nisi to go through.

However, when a 'friend' told her that her husband was having an affair with a woman down the road, she saw red. At 3 am one morning, she crept to the house of his mistress, Amanda Acheson, and poured five litres of white gloss paint over his precious BMW car, which was parked outside.

She then returned to the former marital home in East Garston, Berkshire, and chopped the sleeves off three cashmere coats and 32 Savile Row bespoke-tailored suits. Finally, her rampage ended when she delivered the contents of her husband's vintage wine cellar, including bottles of Chateau Latour 61 worth £300 per bottle, to the neighbours' doorsteps.

Lady Graham-Moon was later quoted as saying that she had been driven to revenge by the fact that her husband had been conducting his affair 'right on my doorstep'.

## At the Third Stroke ...

A jilted woman used her ex-lover's mobile phone to call the speaking clock. He was presented later with a bill for £500.

## Curtain Poles

This one may be loosely based on a true story but has now moved into the realm of the urban myth.

She spent the first day packing her belongings into boxes, crates and suitcases. On the second day, she had the removal firm collect her things. On the third day, she sat down for the last time at their beautiful dining room table by candlelight, put on some soft background music, and feasted on a pound of prawns, a jar of caviar and a bottle of Chardonnay.

When she had finished, she went into each and every room and stuffed half-eaten prawn shells, dipped in caviar, into the hollow of all of the curtain poles. She then cleaned up the kitchen and left.

When the husband returned with his new girlfriend, all was bliss for the first few days.

Then slowly, the house began to smell. They tried everything: cleaning, mopping, and airing the place out. Vents were checked for dead rodents, and carpets were steam cleaned, air fresheners were hung everywhere. Exterminators were brought in to set off gas canisters, during which they had to move out for a few days, and in the end they even paid to replace the expensive wool carpeting.

Nothing worked. People stopped coming over to visit. Repairmen refused to work in the house. The maid quit. Finally, they could not take the stench any longer and decided to move.

A month later, even though they had cut their price in half, they couldn't find a buyer for their stinky house. Word got out, and eventually, even the local estate agents refused to return their calls. Finally, they had to borrow a huge sum of money from the bank to purchase a new place.

The ex-wife called the man, and asked how things were going. He told her the saga of the rotting house. She listened politely, and said that she missed her old home terribly, and would be willing to reduce her divorce settlement in exchange for getting the house back.

Assuming that his ex-wife had no idea how bad the smell was, he agreed on a price that was about a tenth of what the house had been worth, but only if she'd sign the papers that very day. She agreed, and within the hour his lawyers delivered the paperwork.

A week later the man and his girlfriend stood smiling as they watched the moving company pack everything to take to their new home … including the curtain poles.

*Don't you just love happy endings?*

## Stuck on You

A 16-year-old girl in Harrisburg, Pennsylvania was charged with assault in July 2000 for gluing her cheating boyfriend's penis to his abdomen. The girl claimed she meant it as a joke, but the boyfriend wound up in the hospital and the juvenile authorities were not amused.

## Haute Cuisine

A wife who had been treated badly by her domineering and philandering husband walked the streets during the day collecting dog excrement in a bag.

When she had enough, she put it in a pan, added onions, stock and herbs, and made a dog poop casserole. She reports that, after eating the dish, her unwitting husband proclaimed how much he'd enjoyed it.

## Stitched up?

One Saturday lunchtime in 1975, a group of friends were doing their best to see how many beers they could down before closing time at 3 pm. When the pub kicked them out, they congregated on the pavement outside and one of them started making rude gyrations with his body at passing females. Two passing policemen spotted the antics and promptly arrested a different member of the group. He was taken to the police station, proclaiming his innocence, but to no avail. He was locked up.

His friends let his wife know what had happened so she wasn't worried by his non-appearance at home at the expected time. She wasn't impressed, although she accepted their explanation of his innocence.

At 6 pm, the detainee was released on police bail, but instead of heading home, he decided he needed another drink, so the gang returned to the pub where they stayed until closing time at 11 pm.

Unbeknown to them, his wife had phoned the police station at 6.05 pm to ask when her husband would be released and had been told that he'd already left. As the evening progressed and he still hadn't shown up, she decided to get even with her missing husband who was something of a Beau Brummel, and had a penchant for fashionable, expensive clothes.

Next morning, when he got up nursing a bad hangover, he went to the wardrobe and selected an outfit for the day. When he tried to button his shirt, he found that every buttonhole had been sewn tightly shut. As had every buttonhole on every shirt, jacket, coat and pair of trousers he possessed (a considerable number).

Over the coming weeks, he spent hours carefully unpicking all the immaculate stitching, trying to avoid damaging his expensive items of clothing.

He never, ever repeated his mistake.

## Sharp Shooting

In February 2000, the *Weekly World News*, an American tabloid newspaper, carried the story of 'gun-toting granny' Ava Estelle of Melbourne, Australia. Apparently, the 81-year-old grandmother was so angry when two thugs raped her 18-year-old granddaughter that she tracked the unsuspecting ex-cons down – and shot their testicles off!

The feature reports, 'Cops say convicted rapist and robber Davis Furth, 33, lost both his penis and his testicles when outraged Ava opened fire with a 9 mm pistol in the seedy hotel room where he and former prison cellmate Stanley Thomas, 29, were holed up.

'The wrinkled avenger also blew Thomas' testicles to kingdom come, but doctors managed to save his mangled penis, police said.'

*Although this story appeared in a national newspaper and is still being passed around as factual, it has actually now been debunked as an urban myth.*

## Ripping Yarns

When his Venezuelan girlfriend returned home to find a London DJ in bed with his new love, she flew into a rage and cut up all his suits with a pair of scissors.

## Airbrushed Smile?

After being dumped in a most callous way, a woman took the opportunity before leaving the house of cleaning her ex-partner's toilet with his toothbrush. She often speculates whether he now has some dreadful gum disease.

# Girl-on-Girl Revenge Action

Women seem to reserve their most vengeful acts for the men in their lives, but when they do decide to get even with another female, it's always spectacularly devious.

Anyone who has seen the black comedy film *Death Becomes Her* starring Meryl Streep and Goldie Hawn will have some insight into the lengths women might go to in order to pull a fast one over a rival. In the film, actress Madeline Ashton (Meryl Streep) steals nerdish plastic surgeon Ernest Menville (Bruce Willis) from her long-time friend and rival Helen (Goldie Hawn). Both women, eager to stay young forever, visit a mysterious woman (Isabella Rossellini) who gives them a potion for eternal youth. Between them, both Hawn and Streep find ways to torment and terrorise the other in ever-increasing acts of reprisal. They both end up 'dead' and needing plastic surgeon Willis to keep their bodies together. The Machiavellian plot is outlandish and hilarious, but the most believable part is the conniving way in which the women get even with each other.

## Dressed to Kill

Jennifer's wedding day was fast approaching. Nothing could dampen her excitement – not even her parents' nasty divorce. Her mother had found the *perfect* dress to wear and would be the best-dressed mother-of-the-bride ever!

A week later, Jennifer was horrified to learn that her father's new young wife had bought exactly the same dress. Jennifer asked her to exchange it, but she refused.

'Absolutely not. I look like a million bucks in this dress, and I'm wearing it,' she replied.

Jennifer told her mother who graciously said, 'Never mind sweetheart. I'll get another dress. After all, it's your special day.'

A few days later, they went shopping and did find another gorgeous dress. When they stopped for lunch, Jennifer asked her mother, 'Aren't you going to return the other dress? You really don't have another occasion where you could wear it.' Her mother just smiled and replied, 'Of course I do, dear. I'm wearing it to the rehearsal dinner the night before the wedding!'

## Over to You

When this particular cuckolded woman who lived in Surrey reached her mid-sixties, she decided to make a few changes; her family had all grown up and left home and, on discovering that her husband had been having an ongoing affair for many years while she had been working hard to run the family business and to bring up the family, she decided she should do something about it.

Her husband had recently developed a heart problem and was advised by his GP to take things easy. Instead of tea and sympathy, it was at this point that the wife told him to pack his things and to go and live with his lady friend. As she pointed out, why should she nurse him through his (and her) old age and health problems when his mistress had had the best years? By her reckoning, if the lady friend had enjoyed the best of him, she could have the rest of the years of illness as well.

## Who's Laughing Now?

In the United States, a wife found out that her husband had been having an affair. Nonetheless, the couple were keen to try to make the marriage work and were trying to sort out their problems. However, the mistress continued to contact the husband. So the wife decided to get revenge on the 22-year-old mistress who made a habit of seducing married men. She said, 'Mine was certainly not the first husband she'd seduced, and probably won't be the last. She confessed that she likes it.'

The husband agreed to be in on the act of vengeance. He phoned the ex-mistress in a frantic state, saying that the wife had gone crazy. In the background, the wife was shouting and screaming. In the middle of the warning, the mistress heard her ex-lover scream, 'No, don't shoot!' A gun goes off together with crazed laughter.

Moments later, the wife takes the phone and tells the mistress that she is going to kill herself and leave a suicide note explaining why with her name on it. Apparently, the mistress had a very upsetting and uncomfortable few hours while she waited for the police to show up – and of course they never came. Whether she mended her ways is not known but she left the 'vengeful' couple alone thereafter.

## Expensive Date

Hell hath no fury like someone promised a husband who fails to get one.

Anne Majerik, a 60-year-old widow from Pennsylvania, has successfully sued the world's most expensive match-maker, Orly Hadida, after she failed to produce an eligible 'cultured gentleman' worth 'up to $20 million' for her.

The Beverly Hills matchmaker charges anywhere up to $200,000 to find a suitable husband for applicants but she was unable to find 'Mr Right' for Ms Majerik who paid $125,000 for the service.

Ms Hadida counter-sued in the civil court, saying that her former client was 'a terrible date' and also that she was a 'serial matchmaker suer'.

The court finally ruled in favour of Ms Majerik, award-ing her $2.1 million (£1.1 million), if somewhat reluctantly. Christie Troutt, the jury foreman, was quoted as saying, 'We wanted to punish the defendant, but in the amount, we wanted to punish the defendant but we didn't want to reward the plaintiff. They were both wrong.'

# Boudicca

Perhaps the most famous woman avenger of all time was Boudicca, a queen of the ancient Britons, who led the revolt against the Romans. She was a fearsome warrior and not prepared to take an insult lying down. Her story is as follows:

After the death of her husband Prasutagus who together with Boudicca ruled over the Iceni tribe in East Anglia under Roman authority, the Romans heaped humiliation upon humiliation on the Celtic queen by imposing heavy taxes, conscription and demands for land.

The queen refused and, to set an example to other tribes and to break her spirit, Boudicca and her two daughters were publicly flogged and the daughters raped. This was the final insult.

Boudicca determined to exact her revenge on Nero and his legions and to oust the Romans from Britain. She raised an army and marched on the new Roman town of Colchester. Other tribes joined her revolt, also keen to teach the Romans a lesson, and after sacking Colchester, the army led by Boudicca marched on London and St Albans.

# Female Revenge

Those tribes that stayed loyal to the Romans (like the Catuvellauni) were also subject to Boudicca's wrath.

The Roman Governor General Suetonius Paulinus and his troops finally faced Boudicca and her army of Britons in the field somewhere in the Midlands. It was a desperate pitched battle, and although the Romans were eventually victorious, there were high casualties on both sides.

Many thousands of Britons fell in battle and the survivors were hunted down and killed by Roman soldiers. Boudicca survived but the defeat was too much for the proud warrior queen who took her own life by drinking poison.

Nonetheless, although ultimately defeated, Boudicca's defiance and revenge attacks brought the Roman world up short and she very nearly succeeded in ousting the invaders. From that point on, the Romans are said to have treated the native Celtic people with a little more respect so, from that point of view, her act of revenge was not in vain.

# Domestic Bliss?

They say no one knows what goes on behind closed doors – and it's true that even the most harmonious of couples probably have the odd bust-up in private, but the following stories are about husband and wife teams who take a disagreement one step further.

## Can I Help?

After being made redundant a few times during the 1980s, Julian Temple started his own business. His wife had been the UK's international marketing manager for Reebok but, on having children, she had decided to leave her job to be a stay-at-home mum.

Julian says, 'As my business was in its infancy, I was stressed most of the time. I was preparing for an international trade exhibition, and the day before I left I was more than a bit pressed for time. My wife asked if there was anything she could do to help. I think she was expecting a commission to do some strategic international marketing consultancy – but my answer was, "Well, my shirts could do with ironing." This was obviously not the answer she expected.

She said nothing. My shirts were pressed and immaculate when they were presented to me – along with the bill from the ironing service!'

## No Rest for the Wicked

On the *Today* programme on BBC Radio 4, a vicar told the story of one of his parishioners who had her husband's ashes placed in an egg timer. She reasoned that he'd been a lazy so-and-so while alive so she thought she'd put him to work once dead.

## What a Blast

A long-suffering wife was sick and tired of her husband mending his motorcycles in the house but he persisted in his loutish ways.

On this particular day, the guy pushed his motorcycle from the patio into the living room where he began to clean the engine with a rag and a bowl of petrol. Once cleaned to his satisfaction, he sat on the bike and decided to start it to make sure everything was OK. Unfortunately, the bike was in gear, and it crashed through the glass patio door with him still on it.

His wife ran to his aid but he was badly cut from the shards of broken glass. She called 911, and the paramedics took him to hospital. He was stitched and patched in Accident & Emergency and sent home to bed. The wife cleaned up the mess in the living room and poured the bowl of petrol down the toilet.

Later that afternoon, the husband woke up, lit a cigarette and went to the lavatory. He sat down and tossed the cigarette between his legs into the toilet bowl – which instantly exploded because his wife hadn't flushed the petrol away. The explosion blew the hapless fellow through the bathroom door.

On hearing the explosion and her husband's screams, the wife ran into the hall and found him lying groaning on the floor with his trousers blown away and burns to his buttocks. Once again, the wife rang the emergency services.

Coincidentally, the same two paramedics arrived at the scene. They loaded the husband on to a stretcher and began carrying him to the waiting ambulance. However, when they asked the wife how his injuries had been sustained, they laughed so much that they dropped the stretcher and broke the man's collarbone.

*If that's not karmic revenge for repairing a motorbike in the lounge, what is?*

## Fax Stranger than Fiction

Julian Temple, a British businessman, took the afternoon departure from the UK to Dubai. The Emirates on-board hospitality was extremely good and he enjoyed the food and the wine. On arrival in Dubai, he was a bit inebriated. The flight arrived midnight local time, but the queue for passport control was extremely long.

It was four hours ahead of UK time, so he decided to ring home. His wife answered the phone but his squiffy greeting – while she was juggling two children under the age of three and an absent husband – was met with a real ear-bashing.

At first, he tried to smooth things over and to reason with her but to no avail. Even in his squiffy state, he could still understand that it was, at £2.50 per minute, an expensive tongue-lashing he was paying for. So, unwisely as it turned out, he simply closed the mobile and switched it off.

The intoxicated traveller finally made it through customs and to his hotel. Just as he was dosing off to sleep, he heard an envelope being delivered under his bedroom door. As he was expecting some critical business issue, he got up and opened the envelope.

The cover sheet on the fax read:

To: Mr J Temple
From: Mrs E Temple

The fax ran to 32 pages, but from then on it was blank – because his wife was not speaking to him!

But her revenge had a final twist. When the man checked out of the hotel a week later, his bill included a charge for receiving a 32-page fax. Taking the mobile phone call would have been cheaper!

## Never Try to Outsmart a Woman!

A wife who had spent all her married life living with a miserly husband was faced with a dilemma. Before he died, the penny-pinching husband had made the wife promise that when he died, she would bury all his money with him in the coffin. She had tried to remonstrate with him but he was insistent. As a devout Christian, she felt she had to honour her promise when her parsimonious husband finally died.

She thought long and hard about it and finally came up with a solution. She put all his money into her account and wrote him a cheque, which she duly put into the coffin with the dead man! Her reasoning, 'If he can cash it, he can spend it.'

*This story is being sent around by email as a true story but this cannot be substantiated at the moment.*

## Hell Hath No Fury like a Woman Scorned

The following victims of revenge made the mistake of neglecting their women or, worse, ignoring their needs. As you can see, women can only be pushed so far before their pride demands action ...

## His Pride and Joy

Wife of radio DJ Tim Shaw saw red when he told the model Jodie Marsh on air that he was prepared to leave his wife and their two children for her, reported *Metro*. His wife Hayley, who was listening to his show, immediately posted an advert for his £25,000 Lotus Esprit Turbo sports car on eBay with a 'Buy It Now' option of 50p.

The item description read: 'I need to get rid of this car in the next two to three hours before my husband gets home to find it gone and all his belongings in the street.'

The car sold within five minutes.

The DJ had upset his wife previously on air by telling her sister that he thought about her while having sex with his pregnant wife. Mrs Shaw said: 'I am sick of him disrespecting this family for the sake of his act.

'The car is his pride and joy but the idiot put my name on the logbook so I just sold it. I didn't care about the money, I just wanted to get him back.'

*This story has echoes around the world – we had reports of a wife in New Zealand whose husband left her for another woman. He called to tell her to sell his prize Corvette and send him the money. Next thing the neighbours saw was the car with a huge sign on it – 'FOR SALE $20' – and you can see the American version in Chapter 5, Motoring Revenge!*

## Not Tonight, Josephine

A 52-year-old woman from Buenos Aires stabbed her husband in the back – literally – because he refused to have sex with her. Thankfully, the inattentive husband was not seriously injured.

Apparently, the woman had spent all day trying to get her husband into bed but he had ignored all her seductions. The spurned wife told *La Cuarta* newspaper: 'I wore a G-string and high heels in the house but he didn't notice. I couldn't stand this. I got really mad and I stabbed him.'

The husband went straight to the police to report the crime before going to the hospital to have his wounds treated.

The police spokesman expressed some surprise that the woman didn't seem to think she had done anything wrong: 'She kept saying that he was her husband and that he had to fulfil his obligations and, because he didn't, she had the right to punish him.'

## Pushing His Luck

When an unfaithful husband in Thailand asked his wife to make love one last time before he left her for another woman, his wife was not amused. In fact, she was so unimpressed that she cut off her husband's penis and tossed it over the fence in the front garden.

Saithong Wantha, 53, then called neighbours to take her

husband, Udom Phorit, 35, to hospital while she turned herself in to the police, reports *The Nation* newspaper.

Unfortunately, the neighbours couldn't find the missing organ so they had to call Saithong on her mobile phone in order to locate it.

There was a two-hour wait before surgeons at Khon Kaen University's Srinakharin Hospital could operate. However, the penis was successfully reattached although they said there was only a 50:50 chance it would function properly.

Saithong's reasoning for her vengeful rage – she wanted to stop him philandering and she thought that if he could no longer function sexually, he might stay with her.

*Weird logic but, hey, perhaps he shouldn't have pushed his luck with that one last request.*

## Wakey Wakey

It's not just wives who expect their lovers to perform ... when a Romanian man fell asleep while making love to his mistress, she took it as a huge insult. To teach the man a lesson, she inserted his penis through his wedding ring. The patient, who was married with two children, had to go to hospital to have the wedding ring removed.

## What a Babe

A farmer from a small rural community in Cumbria was unfaithful to his wife with one of his pigs. During the sex act, unluckily for him, the farmer became stuck fast. Despite his best efforts, he could not withdraw from the pig so he had to call his wife for help.

Rather than save his blushes, the enraged wife called the local fire brigade and made sure all the details of the incident were known.

The firemen turned up mob-handed to laugh at the man's misfortune and to commiserate with his wife.

## Just Say No

When Svetin Gulisija, 26, from Seget in Croatia decided to light a fire in woods behind his house because he was too tired for sex with his wife, he could not have imagined how badly things could go wrong.

Firstly, the pair had to be evacuated when his home caught fire (the damage was estimated at around £15,000) and then, he was jailed for two years for arson.

# The Last Laugh

## Wedding Anniversary Sex

A husband and his wife had a bitter quarrel on the day of their 40th wedding anniversary. The husband yelled, 'When you die, I'm getting you a headstone that reads: "Here Lies My Wife – Cold As Ever".'

'Yeah,' she replied, 'When you die, I'm getting you a head-stone that reads: "Here Lies My Husband – Stiff At Last".'

## Genie's Wish

After her recent divorce, a wife is granted three wishes by a genie. However, the catch is that whatever she wishes for, her ex-husband will receive the same but doubled.

Initially, she wishes for £10 in her purse. Sure enough, when she opens her purse, £10 is there and her ex-husband smugly confirms he has £20 in his wallet.

Next, she wishes for £1 million. She duly gets it and her gleeful ex gets £2 million.

After careful thought, she asks the genie, 'I wish I was half-dead!'

## Dirty Trick

'Cash, cheque or charge account?' the shop assistant asked, after folding the items the woman wished to purchase.

As she fumbled for her purse, the assistant noticed a remote control for a television set in her handbag.

'So, do you always carry your TV remote?' she asked.

'No,' replied the woman, 'but my husband refused to come shopping with me, and I thought this was the most evil thing I could do to him legally.'

## Bedside Vigil

Jake was dying. His wife, Becky, was maintaining a candle-light vigil by his side.

She held his fragile hand, tears running down her face. Her praying roused him from his slumber; he looked up and his pale lips began to move slightly.

'Becky, my darling,' he whispered.

'Hush, my love,' she said. 'Rest, don't talk.'

He was insistent. 'Becky,' he said in his tired voice, 'I have something that I must confess.'

'There's nothing to confess,' replied the weeping Becky, 'Everything's all right, go to sleep.'

'No, no. I must die in peace, Becky. I … I slept with your sister, your best friend, her best friend and your mother!'

'I know, sweetheart,' whispered Becky, 'let the poison work.'

## Mad Wife Disease

A guy was sitting quietly reading his paper when his wife walked up behind him and whacked him on the head with a magazine.

'What was that for?' he asked.

'That was for the piece of paper in your trousers' pocket with the name Laura Lou written on it,' she replied.

'Two weeks ago when I went to the races, Laura Lou was the name of one of the horses I bet on,' he explained.

'Oh darling, I'm sorry,' she said. 'I should have known there was a good explanation.'

Three days later he was watching the football on TV when she walked up and hit him on the head again, this time with the iron frying pan, which knocked him out cold. When he came to, he asked, 'What the hell was that for?'

She replied, 'Your horse called.'

# Cake or Bed

A husband is at home watching a football game when his wife interrupts, 'Dear, could you fix the light in the hallway? It's been flickering for weeks now.'

He looks at her and says angrily, 'Fix the lights now? Does it look like I have Powergen written on my forehead? I don't think so.'

'Fine.' Then the wife asks, 'Well then, could you fix the fridge door? It won't close properly.' To which he replies, 'Fix the fridge door? Does it look like I have Comet written on my forehead? I don't think so.'

'Fine,' she says, 'then you could at least fix the steps to the front door? They are about to break.'

'I'm not a carpenter and I don't want to fix steps.' He says, 'Does it look like I have B&Q written on my forehead? I don't think so. I've had enough of you. I'm going to the pub!' So he goes to the pub and drinks for a couple of hours.

He starts to feel guilty about how he treated his wife, and decides to go home. As he walks into the house, he notices that the steps are already fixed. As he enters the house, he sees the hall light is working. As he goes to get a beer, he notices the fridge door is fixed. 'Darling,' he asks, 'How did all this get fixed?'

She said, 'Well, when you left I sat outside and cried. Just then a nice young man asked me what was wrong, and I told him. He offered to do all the repairs, and all I had to do was either go to bed with him or bake a cake.'

He said, 'So what kind of cake did you bake?'

She replied, 'Hellooooo … Do you see Jane Asher written on my forehead? I don't think so!'

# Chapter Two

# Male Revenge

*'When a man steals your wife, there is no better
revenge than to let him keep her.'*
Sacha Guitry,
Russian playwright (1885–1957)

When researching the stories for this book, a very clear
trend became apparent: for every story that I found
about a man seeking revenge, I found at least ten stories
of women seeking revenge. The only difference was that
women appear to seek revenge almost exclusively on ex-
lovers and former partners whom they feel have 'done 'em
wrong' whereas when men resort to acts of revenge, the
target can be anyone … cheating wives, irritating neighbours, ungrateful bosses – you name it.

However, a recent study by University College, London,
published in *Nature*, flies in the face of my findings. The
UCL series of experiments was designed to make vol-
unteers dislike strangers who had offended them and to

gauge their brain's reactions when the culprits experienced mild pain. What the research findings show is that women exhibit empathy for those people they both liked and disliked. Conversely, lead researcher Dr Tania Singer says, 'Men expressed more desire for revenge and seemed to feel satisfaction when unfair people were given what they perceived as deserved physical punishment.'

You have been warned! Men like to get even too, as the following stories show.

# Jilted John ...

The pages of novels are littered with men who have been driven mad with rage and jealousy by their cheating wives and who thereafter sought to kill their rival in love. In fact, this theme has been around since the time of the Greek tragedies, most notably perhaps in the tale of Helen of Troy. When the legendary beauty ran off with another man (Paris), her husband Menelaus not only followed her to get her back, but he instigated the ten-year Greek war against the Trojans, commonly known as the Trojan War.

Perhaps the following cuckolded husbands and lovers have not gone that far but they certainly were not the types to turn the other cheek either!

## A Bit of a Do

A wedding party in Varazdin, Croatia went horribly wrong when doctors had to be called to separate the bride and best man when they were caught in the act. The couple were trapped together by a muscle spasm after a friend of the groom walked in on them as they had sex in the toilets.

Unable to separate, the couple were subjected to a procession of wedding guests who came to see what all the fuss was about before the doctors arrived.

The still-entangled pair were put on a stretcher and taken to the local hospital where the bride was given an injection to relax her muscles, so allowing the best man to withdraw.

Meanwhile, back at the hotel, the groom decided to make the best of it and asked guests to continue to enjoy the party, which was now to celebrate his impending divorce, according to daily newspaper *Slobodna Dalmacija*.

## That Sinking Feeling

Spurned husband Mark Bridgwood is alleged to have used an axe to sink his £100,000 yacht, *Rebel*, when he found out that his ex-wife Tracey had advertised it for £40,000 for 'a quick sale' in the Torquay-based *Herald Express* after the couple had argued.

The 35-foot ketch sank in Dartmouth harbour leaving only parts of the two masts above water. After police ruled out criminal charges, saying 'it is a matter for the harbour authorities', the couple were asked to meet the £100,000 cost of the salvage operation by the Dartmouth harbour master.

*No winners there, then.*

## Wedding Speech

A young man knew of his fiancée's infidelity but, rather than breaking off the relationship, he kept quiet until the day of the wedding when, during his groom's speech, he told the assembled guests of his new wife's unfaithful behaviour – and to top it all, it was with his best friend, in fact, the best man.

With that, he turned to his wife and told her that he wanted a divorce – and left.

## Because You're Worth It

A young man in Surrey had a live-in girlfriend who was very keen on fashion and beauty. She had expensive clothes and the best cosmetic products.

He had suspicions that she was being unfaithful. When he was presented with the evidence, he decided to hit her where it would hurt … in her beauty regime. So each morning when he showered, he would urinate in her expensive shampoo and conditioner bottles.

## Martin Scissorhands

When his girlfriend Vikki Hewett, 27, left him, Martin Walker, 31, flew into a rage and cut up all six of her new bikinis in order to ruin her holiday, reported *The Times* newspaper.

## The Naked Truth

The *Mirror* newspaper reported that a husband from Wales took revenge on his unfaithful ex-wife by selling 200 sexy photos of her on eBay. Apparently, the man offered the CD pictures of the 24-year-old blonde at £4.99 each and they had all gone within 24 hours.

The seller posted a message on the internet site, saying, 'She was playing away with my so-called best friend and now it's payback time.'

# I Can't Take it Any More

Sometimes a long-held grudge niggles away at a man and he stews on it for years. Then something seemingly innocent happens and it triggers an over-the-top and completely out-of-all-proportion act of retribution.

## Fridge Raider

*New York Times* reporter and author Ian Urbina tells in his book called *Life's Little Annoyances* the story of when he finally snapped after one of his three room-mates kept eating his ice-cream. He didn't know which one, so he bought a container of Ben & Jerry's, skimmed off the top layer and replaced it with a layer of salt which, when frozen, looks like ice cream, and put it in the shared fridge.

A few days later, he got an email from the ice-cream thief but, instead of being full of remorse for stealing and for being caught, the culprit berated Urbina for being inconsiderate and for not being more understanding of her condition – which it transpires was an irresistible urge to eat ice cream whenever she saw it.

## Protective Dad

A father who had been taken to the cleaners by his ex-wife remained civil to her and the new boyfriend for the sake of his children. However, the new man in her life took great pleasure in flaunting his victory – not least by showing off his new, swanky car ... but the ex realised it had no tax, insurance or MOT.

The New Man laughed at the ex-husband when he warned him not to drive it with his kids in it. So he told the police where and when to find him one day. They pulled the show-off over and arrested him (after all, they already had his name and address). The car was crushed (as were his dreams) and the man received a £1,000 fine plus costs.

*Who's the Daddy?*

## On the Treadmill

A news report told of a practical joker in the US who got his come-uppance when his long-suffering friends turned the tables by converting his apartment into a hamster cage, complete with shredded newspaper, a 6-foot exercise wheel and a giant water bottle.

Over the years, Luke Trerice, 28, had constantly played pranks and practical jokes on his friends. So, finally, one friend, Chris Kirk, decided to plot his revenge.

With the help of other victims of Trerice's pranks, Chris and the team bought the materials costing US$300 (£161) to make the hamster conversion. The job took eight people 100 hours each.

Trerice says he is going to keep the wheel, and is already planning a counter-attack.

## Clean Your Room or Else!

After repeatedly asking his 20-year-old daughter Claire to clean up her room, father Steve Williams finally got so fed that he sought drastic measures. Finally, he posted a photograph of Claire's messy bedroom on his own website, www.shameit.com.

Claire was suitably shamefaced and has tidied her room. Given the success of his shock tactics, Mr Williams' website now offers other people the chance to share cringeworthy antics caught on camera.

## Vulgar Boatman

In the 1960s, the man in charge of renting out the boats on Newcastle upon Tyne's Exhibition Lake was consistently unpleasant to the schoolboys who liked to hire the rowing boats. One day, some of these boys took out three boats. They rowed to the opposite end of the lake and moored them.

The boatman blew his whistle and called them in, but instead they ran off.

The man was obliged to shut his hut and to row across the lake to retrieve his missing boats.

The guilty boys were subsequently banned, but they adjudged it worthwhile for the aggravation they had caused the officious boatman.

## Mistaken Identity

After years of stewing resentment and pain suffered after a dentist allegedly pulled out the wrong teeth in 1992 and then botched the repair work, a 47-year-old German man from Bielefeld had had enough. He'd been on a heavy drinking session and decided the time was right to drive to the dental surgery to tell the dentist what he thought of him.

Unfortunately, he mistook a dentist who was leaving the surgery after work for the alleged perpetrator of the bodged dental work, and then on the spur of the moment decided to run him down.

German police said it was a miracle that the injured dentist suffered only cuts and bruises and had not been killed. While the original dentist escaped Scot free, the defendant – who admitted trying to kill him – faced charges of attempted manslaughter and grievous bodily harm.

## Festive Cheer

One Christmas, a teenage boy received a box of six mince pies as a gift. He put them in the fridge and told his little brother not to touch them. After a couple of days, he discovered that three had been eaten. So he ate one of his mince pies and told his little brother to leave the remaining two alone – or else.

But did he listen? No. The next day, another mince pie was missing. Rather than gobble down the last mince pie, the older brother decided to teach his little brother a lesson. He carefully lifted the lid of the remaining pie, scooped out the mincemeat and replaced it with mustard. He then replaced the top and put it back in the box.

Sure enough, the little brother took a massive bite from the mince pie before discovering his mouth-blistering mistake.

## Buzz Words

After a long-running neighbour dispute, one of the parties went on holiday for two weeks in the summer. The other neighbour took advantage of their absence to put two pints (yes, they do sell them by the pint for anglers) of maggots through the neighbour's letterbox. The family returned to a Hitchcock-like house of flies … yuk!

## Cleaning Row

Cleaning rotas are the bane of many flatmates' lives, but 22-year-old Andrew Percy took things a step too far when he fell out with his two female flatmates after they asked him to clean the bathroom.

*The Times* newspaper reported that Percy, who worked at Newcastle General Hospital's Accident & Emergency department, is facing jail for putting bleach in his former flatmates' milk.

Fortunately, the two women noticed a bitter taste when they drank their tea and ate their breakfast cereal, and so they called the police. When arrested, Percy admitted that he had done a 'stupid' thing.

*Master of the understatement, methinks.*

## Stamp it Out

A family had grown thoroughly tired of a neighbour who allowed his dog to foul on their front garden. So, one day, the teenage son and his mate collected the poop in a bag, rang the neighbour's doorbell and, as he approached, set fire to the bag on the doorstep.

The man answered the door and immediately stamped on the flaming bag to put it out.

*Squelch!*

## Revenge's Silver Lining

Ferruccio Lamborghini was a wealthy tractor manufacturer both before and after World War II and he was a keen sports car enthusiast who, among other cars, drove a Ferrari. The story goes that when the clutch failed on the Ferrari, he took it back to the Ferrari factory, pointing out that it had the same components as the ones he used on his tractors. He approached Enzo Ferrari with his criticisms but the Ferrari founder refused to see him, saying, 'A tractor manufacturer could never be expected to understand high-bred sports cars.'

Lamborghini, having fixed his own clutch with surprising ease, then vowed revenge and so set up his own rival sports car manufacturer close to the Ferrari factory.

Lamborghini enjoyed huge success with his sports cars, especially the famous Countach, and there are those who claim that his first 'revenge' car, the Lamborghini 350GT, was superior to its Ferrari counterpart (the one Lamborghini tried to get fixed) in many, many ways.

# Father of the Pride

It seems that many men have a problem with authority figures. Or, put more simply, men don't like being told what to do. You often hear wives discussing how their suggestions are dismissed out of hand, but if a wife is clever enough to make her husband think that he came up with the original idea it is adopted without resistance.

Obviously, in the normal course of daily events, people are not able to take the time to gently persuade men that they are in control – and both genders are guilty of denting delicate male egos. In some cases this can lead normally mild-mannered men to notions of vile revenge. Having said that, there are very few who actually act on these impulses, but the following collection of stories is of those whose pride had been pricked one time too many ...

## Lawn Aerators

Back in the days before mobile phones, a group of lads got even with an unpopular adult authority figure by targeting his pride and joy – his prize lawn.

# Male Revenge

The young men had insider knowledge, and knew that the proud owner of the pristine lawn was going out one particular afternoon. Before he left, they rang the man saying, 'We're just calling from Hammond United Breweries of Huddersfield to let you know that the van is on its way to put up your new illuminated pub sign.'

The confused man explained that this was a private house but the hoax caller insisted that the address on their docket (ie the man's address) was that of the Collingwood Arms public house. The man was by now getting irate and insisting that his house was not a pub.

The caller sympathised, 'I'm sorry, I can see that there's some mistake but the lads are on their way now and I've no way of contacting them. The first thing they'll do is dig a trench across the lawn to lay the electricity cables for the sign that's going on the edge of your property.'

At this point, the man became completely desperate. The caller replied that he should leave it with him and he'd see what he could do … but, in the meantime, not to go out in case the van arrived in his absence.

The victim of the revenge then had to weigh up whether to cancel his appointment or to leave his precious lawn unattended. In the event, he stayed to guard his lawn but, of course, the fictional lorry never arrived. Goodness only knows how long it took for the poor man's blood pressure to come down.

## Bad News

This story is doing the rounds on the email circuit so it's probably an urban myth – but effective nonetheless.

A domineering and strict father, passing by his son's bedroom, was astonished to see the bed was nicely made, and everything was picked up. Then, he saw an envelope propped up prominently on the pillow. It was addressed, 'Dad'. With the worst premonition, he opened the envelope and read the letter, with trembling hands.

Dear Dad,

It is with great regret and sorrow that I'm writing you. I had to elope with my new girlfriend, because I wanted to avoid a scene with Mom and you. I've been finding real passion with Stacy, and she is so nice, but I knew you would not approve of her, because of all her piercing, tattoos, her tight motorcycle clothes, and because she is so much older than I am. But it's not only the passion ... Dad, she's pregnant. Stacy said that we will be very happy. She owns a trailer in the woods, and has a stack of firewood for the whole winter. We share a dream of having many more children. Stacy has opened my eyes to the fact that marijuana doesn't really hurt anyone.

We'll be growing it for ourselves, and trading it with the other people in the commune, for all the cocaine and ecstasy we want. In the meantime, we'll pray that science will find a cure for AIDS, so Stacy can get better. She sure deserves it!! Don't worry Dad, I'm 15, and I know how to take care of myself. Someday, I'm sure we'll be back to visit, so you can get to know your grandchildren.

Love, your son,

John.

PS Dad, None of the above is true. I'm over at Tommy's house. I just wanted to remind you that there are worse things in life than the report card that's in my centre desk drawer. I love you! Call when it is safe for me to come home.

## Tired and Confused

Two teenage boys held a party while their mother was away for the weekend. On her return, the neighbour complained about the party, her sons and the noise.

So the next time the mother went away, the vengeful boys threw another party – and during the night, they and couple of mates crept next door and took the neighbours gates off their hinges and re-hung them on the opposite side. The gates now looked the same but instead of opening outwards, they opened towards the house and drive.

Next morning, they watched as the unsuspecting neighbour came out to open his gates so he could drive off. The boys were in stitches as the neighbour puzzled over why his gates would no longer swing open and delighted in his obvious confusion and disbelief.

## Literary Heavyweights Come to Blows

When the ever-provocative author Norman Mailer published his anti-feminist book *The Prisoner of Sex* in 1971, he was fully expecting the 'women's libbers' to go after him. However, he was surprised to receive such a cool reception from Gore Vidal, who slated the book in the *New York Review*. When the two writers came face to face on a television show some months later, Mailer was itching for revenge.

Mailer, who was drunk, over-reacted to a touch on the neck from Vidal and tapped his cheek in return. Vidal then slapped Mailer's face, and he in turn head-butted his opponent. They then fought verbally both on and off camera.

It took another twenty years before the two agreed to 'kiss and make up', when *Esquire* magazine paid them to do a joint interview in which Mailer concedes, 'It was a stupid feud in a lot of ways.'

# Slugs and Snails and Puppy-dog Tails

When you read the following tales of revenge involving young men getting their own back on young girls, you can believe the popular nursery rhyme that labels girls as being made of sugar and spice and all things nice while boys comprise slugs, snails and puppy-dog tails!

## Cheers!

Stephen's parents had some friends who were particularly pompous and rather unpleasant to young Stephen. The man was a consultant surgeon and the wife was a member of the Temperance League.

One night, the meeting of the local Temperance League group was being held at this woman's home. While the meeting was underway and under the cover of darkness, Stephen and his friends stealthily dressed out her garden in posters for Guinness and other brands of alcohol.

When the meeting broke up and the ladies left, they were horrified – the busy-body wife never lived down the embarrassment.

## Boys Only Want One Thing

There was a time when a certain type of attractive girl had a reputation for using men to get expensive meals, to get jobs and promotions or to climb social ladders, and certain types of men never seemed to learn – but times, they are a-changing …

A new breed of young men has emerged in London who are now using women, not for their bodies (not even for their expense accounts) but for their cultural cachet. These lifestyle gigolos are purposely seeking out young women in glamorous jobs such as fashion, publishing or film and courting them at opportune times: Fashion Week, Hay-on-Wye, Baftas. After the parties, restaurant openings and film premieres are over, the lifestyle gigolo disappears to look for another good contact.

The Urban Junkies Newsletter warns, 'Guess what, fellas? We're on to you … Our red carpet existence is the result of hard graft … And frankly, we're not prepared to share it any more. From now on: no committed loving relationship, no front row.'

After decades of women using their womanly wiles to get on, the boot seems now to be on the other foot!

## Call and Collect

Two adolescent boys had an exceptionally prissy girl in their class whom they could not stand – and her mother was even worse! Late one Saturday afternoon, the boys telephoned the prissy girl's house and told the mother that they were the parcel office in the centre of town and that there was a large crate waiting for collection marked livestock. Whatever was in the crate was scratching to get out. They insisted that regulations would not allow them to keep livestock in the depot overnight – let alone two nights (the following day being a Sunday) – and could she please come down and collect it straightaway.

The woman was slightly suspicious and asked to speak to the manager. The pair explained that the manager was on his tea break and would be back soon. However, the depot closed in 45 minutes and if she was coming, she'd better come now.

The bluff worked and the prissy mother and her daughter jumped in the car and travelled into town, only to find that the parcel office was not open on a Saturday afternoon and that they had been well and truly set up.

# The Last Laugh

## A Lifetime of Pent-up Resentment

An 80-year-old woman was in front of a judge, charged with shoplifting. He asked her what she'd stolen.

'A can of peaches,' replied the woman.

'How many peaches were in the can?' asked the judge.

She replied that there were six.

'Then I'll give you six days in jail,' said the judge.

Before he had time to speak further, the woman's husband says, 'She also stole a can of peas.'

## Lies and Damned Lies

There was a couple that had been married for 20 years. Every time they made love the husband always insisted on shutting off the light. Well, after 20 years the wife felt this was ridiculous. She figured she would break him out of this crazy habit.

So one night, while they were in the middle of a wild, screaming, romantic session, she turned on the lights. She looked down ... and saw her husband was holding a battery-operated pleasure device ... a vibrator! Soft, wonderful and larger than a real one.

She went completely ballistic.

'You impotent bastard,' she screamed at him, 'How could you be lying to me all of these years? You better explain yourself!'

The husband looks her straight in the eyes and says calmly: 'I'll explain the toy ... you explain the kids.'

## One-upmanship

A man driving a pink and purple Volkswagen Beetle pulls up next to a little man in a Rolls-Royce at the traffic lights. Their windows are open and he yells at the man in the Rolls, 'Have you got a telephone in that Rolls?'

The guy in the Rolls says, 'Yes, of course I do.'

'I got one too … see?' the VW man says.

'Uh, huh, yes, that's very nice.'

'You got a fax machine?' asks the VW man.

'Why, actually, yes, I do.'

'I do too! See? It's right here!' brags the VW man.

The light is just about to turn green and the guy in the Volkswagen says, 'So, do you have a double bed in the back?'

The little man in the Rolls replies, 'NO! Do you?'

'Yep, my double bed is right here in the back, see?' the VW man replies.

The light turns green and the man in the Volkswagen drives off.

Well, the little man in the Rolls is not about to be one-upped, so he immediately goes to a customising shop and orders them to put a double bed in the back of his car.

About two weeks later, the job is finally done. He picks up his car and drives all over town looking for the pink and purple Volkswagen beetle. Finally, he finds it parked at the kerb, so he pulls his Rolls up next to it.

The windows on the Volkswagen are all fogged up and he feels somewhat awkward about it, but he gets out of his newly modified Rolls and taps on the foggy window of the Volkswagen. The man in the Volkswagen finally opens the window a crack and peeks out.

The little man in the Rolls says, 'Hey, remember me?'

'Yeah, yeah, I remember you,' replies the VW man. 'What's up?'

'Look here ... I've got a double bed installed in my Rolls.'

The VW man exclaims, 'YOU GOT ME OUT OF THE SHOWER TO TELL ME THAT?!'

## Wave Goodbye

An elderly couple would constantly argue about everything. The woman often ended the arguments by stating vociferously, 'I'll dance on your grave! I'll dance on your grave!'

Well, sure enough, the old geezer died first.

His last request was that he be buried at sea.

# Chapter Three

# Workplace Revenge

*'Anger ventilated often hurries towards forgiveness;*
*anger concealed often hardens into revenge.'*
Edward G Bulwer-Lytton,
British novelist (1803–80)

Once faceless elements of society, it seems that disgruntled employees have found their voice and are fighting back. A recent survey commissioned in the UK by Novell showed that 58 per cent of employees would continue to use company mobile phones after they'd been given notice at a potential cost to industry of more than £1 million per week, while more than half the Welsh workforce said they would take revenge against a former employer if they were unhappy about losing their job.

Tactics such as continuing to use company benefits, removing company information and exacting revenge on a former employer are all options that have been considered by people if they feel they have been unfairly dismissed.

Yet, it's not just employers who need to be wary – after years of rude and ungrateful treatment, employees are also starting to get their own back on the difficult customer both by direct action and by internet blogs.

And, finally, just when you think the workplace cannot become any more of a jungle, the employers are getting in on the revenge act. Yes, in the United States the number of retaliation charges against employees for filing harassment or discrimination complaints has almost doubled over the last eight years.

But first, let's look at what revenge-bent employees in different sectors of the work force are getting up to.

## Catering Revenge – A Dish Best Served Cold

People who work in the catering trade often receive the worst treatment from ignorant customers, but they are also well placed for dishing out the most unpleasant forms of revenge. After reading the following stories which (be warned) get steadily more gruesome, you'll realise the moral of the story is: never *ever* mess with the people who handle your food, however professional they may seem.

## Fast Food Foul-ups

One disgruntled ex-fast food employee confesses that an innocuous but irritating way to get back at rude customers is, if they order a large coke, to fill the cup three-quarters with ice and then push the small coke button. Another good way to repay rudeness is to leave their burger slightly unwrapped so it falls out when they open it, or by putting the fries in the bag upside-down.

## The Milky Way

William Smith, a milk delivery driver from Penrith who thought his bosses were making him work too many hours, took his revenge by contaminating customers' milk supplies with dog dirt. He hoped that by contaminating the milk, his company would lose orders.

Unfortunately for him, members of the public noticed 'foreign material' and 'grass' in their milk containers and – after a video surveillance operation – the vengeful tamperer was caught.

## Bartender's Retribution Prescription

Bartenders are notorious for hating to make frozen drinks. A US bartender was having trouble with a bunch of young men who regularly gave her a hard time. One guy in particular loved to show his power by asking for frozen cocktails. To add insult to injury, he never tipped.

This particular evening, the guy saw the bartender making some blended drink and asked her what it was she was making. She responded by calling the drink a 'Pain in My Ass'. The guy actually ordered one! Her revenge follows …

While the drink was blending, she poured double doses of prescription laxative into the blender! The trick worked remarkably fast. Within ten minutes, he was running to the toilet.

As the group were getting ready to pay and leave, she noticed that her victim was getting rather anxious again. Being the good bartender she is, she counted back the change as slowly as possible. While counting, she very casually told him, 'Since you never leave me a tip, I have one for you. Don't mess with the bartender!'

## Foaming Ale

An experienced barman who worked at a busy US seafood chain explained that when he has a patron who is behaving badly or tipping poorly, or both, he waits until the offender orders another drink. Then he swishes the glass into the bar cleanser sink, leaving a light coating of the nasty soap-like chemical on the glass. In the case of beer, the chemical results in a nice foamy head and *major* bowel and stomach problems a few hours later.

## Misers Beware

Susannah, a waitress, says on the internet, 'Thank goodness the people who "don't believe" in tipping are few and far between. When I waited tables, I'd sometimes enjoy getting customers who didn't tip, if I already knew who they were, so I could have loads of fun making their service as slow as possible. That satisfaction was worth way more than what their measly tip would've been!'

## Mother's Milk

One very annoying customer who regularly ate at the same restaurant ordered a dessert and one of the waitresses (who happened to just have had a baby) squirted breast-milk into the said dessert. The customer told the waitress that she thought it was delicious!

## Hot Stuff

There are many variations on this theme, but in this particular story from a restaurant in Windsor, the awkward customer kept insisting that he wanted something spicy and that nothing on the menu was fiery enough for his taste.

After moaning on for an eternity, the difficult customer finally chose fajitas. The waitress conveyed the customer's request to the chef who, insulted, decided to spice up the usual fajitas by adding a bottle of Tabasco sauce.

The customer left the restaurant extremely red-faced for more reasons than one!

## Clean Plate?

One chef confessed that after a customer had very rudely asked for his burger 'without any bloody sauce on it', she licked the sauce off the burger with her tongue and then sent it out.

## Fishy Tale

A man who owns a fresh fish shop in London admits that he has an 'involuntary' tip box behind the counter. Customers who are rude or awkward are unknowingly charged a 'service tax' for their bad behaviour, which is collected in the tip box. When the box is full, members of staff are given a meal out, courtesy of the offensive customers.

## Optional Toppings

According to numerous and varying accounts, a common revenge trick in the catering industry is to cough, spit or drop phlegm and other unspeakable bodily fluids into the unsuspecting, tricky customer's meal/drink and then serve it with a smile.

However, the following story which may or may not be apocryphal, has to be the worst case of customer food contamination of all time ...

A woman had sent her steak back to the kitchen on two occasions because it was not cooked to her liking. When it returned the second time, the woman thought that it tasted rather funny and so, suspecting that she may get food poisoning, she took a sample of the steak with her when she left the restaurant.

Sure enough, the woman was unwell that evening, so they got the meat tested to see if it was contaminated with salmonella, e.coli or some other nasty bacteria. However, the infection that was actually detected could not have been expected.

The steak had been contaminated by a human sexually transmitted disease. The only possible explanation was that it had been in contact with the genitalia (at best) of an infected – and presumably vengeful – person.

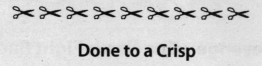

# Done to a Crisp

**An act of revenge with a happy outcome for all ...**

**In 1853, an act of spite led to the invention of one of the most popular snack foods of all time. George Crum was the head chef at Moon's Lake House, a resort in Saratoga Springs, New York. On one particularly fateful day, a customer had the temerity to complain that**

Crum's French fries were 'too thick and soggy' and 'not salty enough'. The angered cook set out to wreak some culinary vengeance. He sliced potatoes paper-thin, fried them to a singed crisped brown, salted the living daylights out of them, and dumped them in front of the hard-to-please diner.

The customer tried one, smiled, then helped himself to the rest of them. Thus were born Saratoga chips, as Crum's unintended invention came to be called. Saratoga chips remained a local delicacy until the Prohibition era, when an enterprising salesman named Herman Lay popularised the product throughout the south-eastern States. Now known as crisps or potato chips, this universally popular snack has spread around the world.

✂ ✂ ✂ ✂ ✂ ✂ ✂ ✂ ✂

# IT Revenge – The Nerds Fight Back

If companies employ clever and innovative IT staff, then they need to be prepared for them to strike back at them in witty and original ways when they become disgruntled or angry.

Of course, computer hacking and destruction of internal company data have been around for years but new forms of revenge attacks are appearing as a result of the widespread use of the internet in the workplace ...

## Bulletin Boards, Chat Rooms and Blogs

The old adage 'the customer is always right' may be the face of the retail trade but privately those in the service or sales industries have always fumed. Now, the downtrodden, silent servers are getting their own back by turning to the web to vent their spleens on rude, arrogant or simply bonkers customers ...

- ✂ Usually those who blog remain anonymous but one vengeful blogger exposed an unwary customer who walked straight into the shop window and bounced off by replaying the in-store video in slow motion for all to see.

- ✂ A day-trader at Lucent Technologies posted a false profit warning on an internet message board and the stock value lost approximately $7 billion from its market value.

- ✂ A disgruntled employee posed as an expert in a chat room and managed to discredit a corporate executive in his former firm against whom he held a grudge.

- ✂ A former employee lashed out at Emulex Corporation by sending a fraudulent internet 'newsletter'. In it, he created a false story claiming that the Emulex CEO was stepping down and that earnings estimates were going to be revised. Subsequently, the price of Emulex's stock fell more than 60 per cent and there was a resulting $2.2 billion loss in market value.

## Server Sabotage

✂ About two weeks after his employment was terminated, Andrew Garcia hacked into his former employer Viewsonic Corporation's computer system and deleted critical files on the server that he used to maintain. The damage meant that workers in the Taiwan office were without computers and vital data for several days.

✂ According to a lawsuit brought by Hewlett-Packard, a former employee sabotaged important tests on one of the new computer servers, giving it lower performance results that cost HP millions of dollars in resources and lost sales.

✂ A computer technician at Forbes Publishing was angered when his temporary position was terminated so he deliberately caused five of eight network servers to crash in retribution. All the data in these servers was deleted and none of it was recoverable. As a result, Forbes was forced to shut down its New York Office for two days and sustained losses of more than $100,000.

## Ticking Bomb

Omega Engineering suffered $10 million in losses when a network engineer, who was unhappy about his job loss, detonated a software time bomb that he had planted on the server that he helped to create.

The bomb paralysed the engineering firm, which manufactures high tech measurement and control devices used by the Navy and NASA, by destroying the programs that ran the company's manufacturing machines.

One day, an employee booted up the central file server that housed more than 1,000 programs and the bomb went off, crashing the server and erasing all programs.

This single act of revenge led to 80 layoffs, and the company says it caused the loss of several of its clients.

## Email Fraud and Spamming

✂ When Diane Kuprewicz lost her job at the School of Visual Arts in New York, she sought vengeance by registering the work email address of the director of human resources on a number of pornographic websites. The director was then deluged by huge numbers of explicit emails for these sites.

✂ A Lockheed Martin employee sent 60,000 colleagues a personal email message requesting an electronic receipt. The result? The whole email system crashed and the company was obliged to fly in a Microsoft emergency team to repair the damage.

✂ Two weeks after he was sacked, a former IT manager of a firm in Silicon Valley gained access to his former employer's email system where he deleted an email server domain, accessed the email account belonging to the president and made configuration changes to the servers so that emails were rejected.

✄ Jason Smathers, a disgruntled AOL software engineer, stole the personal information of 92 million (yes – 92 million!) customers in May 2003 and sold the data to various spammers. Initially, he only charged $28,000 for the data but he soon realised the worth of his ill-gotten gains and began charging $100,000 per sale.

✄ Feeling underpaid and under-valued, an employee of Prudential Insurance exacted his revenge by stealing the electronic personnel files of more than 60,000 Prudential employees. He then sold the information over the internet and, to add insult to injury, he incriminated his former supervisor in the theft.

## Changing Company Websites

A former employee hacked into the company website and posted false information. It took a day to fix the problem, and by then the damage was done. As the CEO (who doesn't want to be identified) confessed, 'Admitting that our website had been hacked into was almost as damaging as the false information that had been put on the site.'

## Creating Critical Websites

✄ After being banned from a Wal-Mart store following an argument with a member of staff, customer

Richard Hatch hired a web design expert and created walmartsucks.org, a site devoted to attacking the retailer.

In just two years, it has sprouted far beyond Hatch's wildest dreams of revenge. More than 1,500 customers have written in to attack rude store managers, complain about alleged insects in the aisles, offer shoplifting tips and, from time to time, write romantic odes to cashiers. Disgruntled employees agitate for unions, expose the purported marital infidelities of supervisors and urge consumers to shop elsewhere. Plaintiffs' lawyers, meanwhile, visit in search of clients and useful evidence against the company.

So it's no surprise that a few months after Hatch opened the site, Wal-Mart's attorneys sent a letter threatening 'necessary action' unless he took it down within 48 hours. Hatch defied the $138 billion retailer – and ultimately Wal-Mart dropped efforts to close the site.

✂ Kourosh Hamidi aimed to 'even the scores' with Intel after he left the company by creating a website critical of Intel and its employment practices.

# Tampering with Internet Phones

✂ A major insurance company lost its voice service for eight hours on about 1,000 internet phone lines because a disgruntled employee introduced a worm that jammed its servers. The crash cost the company hundreds of thousands of dollars.

✄ Sabotage cost a bank an estimated $1 million after a worm infected the voice and data systems. The revenge action effectively closed a trading floor and disabled 500 internet phone lines.

## Shocking IT Statistics

An FBI survey in 2002 showed that 85 per cent of US companies surveyed had a computer intrusion in the last year. Of these, 70 per cent were from people associated with the company.

77 per cent of companies surveyed in the Computer Security Institute/FBI 2003 survey suspected a disgruntled employee as the source of a security breach.

The Gartner Group, the world's largest information technology research and advisory company, reports that 84 per cent of high-cost security incidents occur when insiders send confidential information outside the company.

A 2004 study by the Pokemon Institute shows that the greatest threat to law firm security comes from employee action – whether it is malicious or inadvertent.

## Whistle Blowers

Unhappy or vindictive former employees are getting their own back on employers by turning in the company for using unlicensed software. Richard Saunders, chairman of the British Software Alliance committee in the UK said, 'We definitely receive the most leads from disgruntled employees.'

The BSA's annual piracy figures released in 2006 show that the UK software industry lost £259 million last year because of business software piracy. Companies found using illegal software can be fined and, in a worst-case scenario, a company director can face two years in prison.

It might seem like hitting below the belt, but it seems that blowing the whistle on ex-employers who are abusing piracy laws can be a revenge that hits former employers in the wallet.

✂ ✂ ✂ ✂ ✂ ✂ ✂ ✂ ✂

# General Mayhem

Of course, it's not just those employed in the catering or IT industries that are capable of acts of revenge. Just about any employee is capable of seeing red and turning vengeful.

According to research, there is an unwritten code that governs the working relationship between employer and employee. For example, it is tacitly accepted that employees should get 'fair treatment and a fair day's pay for a fair day's work'.

If this contract is broken – by either party – the employee or employer feels a sense of betrayal as if a formal agreement has been violated – and each side is capable of feeling the same ensuing desire for revenge.

## Helping Yourself

A 40-year-old man was found guilty of theft by a court in Munich, Germany, after he stole almost £5 million from the company he worked for because he had never been given a pay rise. He was caught with the cash stuffed into 40 moneybags in the boot of his car.

The man, who headed a branch of a security firm in Fuerstenfeldbruck near Munich, said he felt mistreated by the company.

The reward for his self-awarded bonus? Four years and three months in prison.

## Airline Staff Reprisals

I once spent a summer working for a European national airline carrier at Heathrow airport. It was common practice for check-in staff to sit rude passengers alongside the fattest person on the flight.

## Kiss & Swell?

In a private school in Ontario, Canada, a caretaker's patience was being sorely tried by a number of 12-year-old girls who insisted on testing their newly purchased lipstick by pressing their lips to the mirror in the girl's toilets, leaving dozens of little lip prints. Despite memos and notices asking the girls to refrain, every night the caretaker would remove the lip marks and the next day the girls would put them back.

Finally, the headmaster agreed to help the caretaker to get his own back on the troublesome girls. She called all the girls to the lavatories and met them there with the caretaker. She explained that all these lip prints were causing a problem for the caretaker who had to clean the mirrors every night. To demonstrate how difficult it was to remove lipstick from the mirrors, she asked the caretaker to show the girls how hard he had to scrub.

Under careful instruction, the man took out a long-handled squeegee, solemnly dipped it in the nearest toilet bowl, and scrubbed at the mirror.

Et voila, *no more lipstick marks.*

## The Emperor's Clothes

The *New York Post* reported that at the Cannes Film Festival in 2005, supermodel Naomi Campbell failed to show up at a charity event organised by her own PR company because her stylist disappeared with her clothes.

Campbell had invited about 50 guests for lunch and a live auction to raise money for Nelson Mandela's Children's Foundation. Campbell is Mandela's honorary granddaughter.

But, when Campbell didn't turn up the event was abandoned. The model's publicist, Rob Shuter, told the *Post*: 'Naomi's stylist disappeared with all her clothes. Naomi had only her underwear. She sat on a boat waiting for two hours for new clothes to arrive. In the end, she borrowed a dress from a girlfriend.'

*Disgruntled employee or 'the dog ate my homework'-style excuse? Who knows?*

## Unexpected Reply

In April 1999, a TV viewer, Jim Neugent, wrote to the ABC television network to complain about the way homosexuality was promoted in its show, *The Practice*. His original email letter of complaint together with ABC's rather unexpected reply is below:

ABC is obsessed (or should I say abscessed) with the subject of homosexuality. I will no longer watch any of your attempts to convince the world that homosexuality is OK. *The Practice* can be a fairly good show but last night's program was so typical of your agenda. You picked the 'dufus' of the office to be the one who was against the idea of his mother being gay and made him look like a whiner because he had convictions.

This type of mentality calls people like me 'gay basher'. Read the first chapter of Romans (that's in the Bible) and see what the apostle Paul had to say about it … He and God and Jesus were all 'gay bashers'.

What if she'd fallen in love with her cocker spaniel … is that an alternative lifestyle? (By the way … the Bible speaks against that, too.)

Jim Neugent

The ABC Online Webmaster replied:

How about getting your nose out of the Bible (which is ONLY a book of stories compiled by MANY different writers hundreds of years ago) and read the Declaration of Independence (what our nation is built on) where it says 'All Men are Created Equal' – and try treating them that way for a change!? Or better yet, try thinking for yourself and stop using an archaic book of stories as your crutch for your existence.

Jim Neugent decided to get even by circulating the webmaster's reply, as he pointed out in his response to ABC:

Thanks for your reply. Evidently, I hit a nerve from your harsh reply. I will share it with all with whom I come in contact. Hopefully, the *Arkansas Democrat Newspaper* will include it in one of their columns.

And I will be praying for you.

Jim Neugent

The employee who penned the original reply was in fact fired by ABC immediately following the incident and the network apologised profusely to Neugent. They also issued the following official email autoresponse to viewers' enquiries:

Subject: RE: technical help

Date: Tues, 27 Apr 1999 19:47:05 − 0400

From: ABC Online Webmaster

Thank you for bringing this to our attention.

We regret that a representative of ABC inappropriately expressed his personal views in response to a viewer's comments, and we sincerely apologize for the disrespectful tone of his answer.

This employee no longer works for the company. We take our viewers' feedback very seriously, as well as their right to express it; and we expect all our employees to do the same.

Thank you for taking the time to write to us.

ABC Online Webmaster

## Salad Days

During a particularly quiet news period in the summer, the editor of breakupgirl.com, who is also a reporter, filed a story for a local magazine about salads in New York restaurants.

The following week, a food critic on a rival magazine wrote a scathing attack on her salad feature. Rather than respond in kind, the journalist got a co-conspirator to deliver one of the salads in question to the critic at his office, with a note reading, 'Dear S., Eat me. Love, L.'

## Forced Labour

A recent inspection of a salvaged Mongolian invasion fleet that sank in a storm in 1281 has revealed that, in all probability, the enslaved Chinese craftsmen, who were dragooned into building the ships purposefully used shoddy workmanship on the Mongolian fleet and this contributed to their destruction in the high seas.

# Will They Notice?

A more subtle and subversive form of revenge is that in which the perpetrator is not looking for instant gratification but will wait to see if anyone notices their seditious acts of reprisal.

## Culture Capital Cock-up

A German town hoping to be named Culture Capital of Europe has just noticed that council workmen laid a swastika in a cobbled street. Apparently, the symbol, which is forbidden in Germany, had been laid into the pavement during 2005 and had remained unnoticed for almost four months until a local resident complained.

The officials at Goerlitz have apologised and are hoping that the revenge trick will not jeopardise their chances of being named Culture Capital for 2010.

## Unappetising Ham

Mick Woods, 34, of Wakefield lost his appetite when he examined the ingredients on a packet of ham and discovered that 'dog s★★t' was listed. Although he and his family found the subversive prank funny, the manufacturers, HR Hargreaves & Son, were less amused. They sacked an employee over the incident and the ham was recalled.

## A Bridge Too Far

A group of young subaltern officers of the Parachute Regiment decided to see how long senior officers would take to notice that a large model of the World War II battle for the bridge at Arnhem had been modified to include a James Bond model car and sundry other items. The additions involved unscrewing the Perspex lid of the large display case to add the items and then reattaching it.

Some months went by, and the prank had been forgotten until some visiting high-ranking foreign dignitaries were being shown around the Mess and one of them asked about the authenticity of an Aston Martin in the World War II reconstruction display, to the great embarrassment of their hosts.

## Funny Scarecrow

At Harvest Festival time, a US restaurant decided to decorate the seating area with stuffed scarecrows, hay, gourds, pumpkins, etc. At every opportunity, the serving staff would pose the scarecrow holding a longish gourd as his penis. It took a while for management to notice, but the customers were quicker on the uptake. The gourds were taken away, so then the staff resorted to putting the scarecrow's hands down his trousers. Eventually the scarecrows were removed.

## Theme Restaurants

A woman diner accidentally walked out of a restaurant leaving her boxed take-away burger on a table, so the waiters decided to place it on top of a large wooden pole that formed part of a nautical-theme display in the middle of the restaurant. It was in clear view of the diners and staff but nobody noticed for some months, despite the growing smell of rotting food.

Eventually, a member of the public pointed it out to the manager. Someone was instructed to get it down immediately – they reported that it was 'rock hard', which is testimony to how long it had been up the pole!

# Unlikely Candidates

It is generally assumed that if anyone in business or trade is likely to wreak revenge, it will be a disgruntled employee – someone who feels impotent and thinks that reprisal is the only course of action left open to them. But you'd be surprised – there are some very unlikely, and sometimes very senior, members of staff who are not above an act of vengeance.

Take the case in May 2001, of Mr Chung, a 24-year-old Princeton graduate who had just started a job with Carlyle in South Korea. He sent a private email to 11 friends at the New York office of Merrill Lynch where he had previously worked. The email was full of bravado about how cushy his new job was and what a success he was with the women.

One of his recipients was obviously not as happy for Mr Chung as the sender had expected and, maliciously or otherwise, passed the email outside the circle of recipients to acquaintances on Wall Street.

It didn't take long before Mr Chung's private message was making the rounds of the financial world, eventually reaching his new bosses at Carlyle. Chung then found himself an ex-employee.

# The Last Laugh

## Pulling Rank

A British Airways passenger cabin was being served by a very camp flight attendant, who seemed to put everyone into a good mood as he served them food and drinks.

As the plane prepared to descend, he came swishing down the aisle and announced to the passengers: 'Captain Marvey has asked me to announce that he'll be landing the big scary plane shortly, lovely people, so if you could just put up your trays that would be super.' On his trip back up the aisle, he noticed that a well-dressed rather exotic-looking woman hadn't moved a muscle. 'Perhaps you didn't hear me over those big brute engines,' he said, 'I asked you to raise your trazy-poo so the main man can pitty-pat us on the ground.' She calmly turned her head and said, 'In my country, I am called a Princess. I take orders from no one.' To which the flight attendant replied, without missing a beat, 'Well, sweet-cheeks, in my country I'm called a Queen, so I outrank you. Tray-up, bitch.'

## Nice Reply

A prominent businessman was on an international flight and tucking into his dinner. Under a lettuce leaf, he found a cockroach, which did not please him.

On his return to base, he wrote a blistering letter of complaint to the airline. Almost by return of post, he received a reply from a devastated managing director, apologising unreservedly for the cockroach incident, saying he'd sacked the whole cabin crew and the flight crew and cancelled the contract with the catering firm.

The businessman, a rather pompous individual, congratulated himself on the power of his complaint. Having some difficulty in putting the letter back into the envelope, he discovered a torn-off part of his letter of complaint, bearing a scrawled note in pencil:

Jane, send this bastard the cockroach letter.

## Touché

A very attractive cabin crew attendant was working in the first class cabin. An older businessman had been eyeing her throughout the flight. Finally, as she passed his seat, he said, 'What would you say to a little f**k?'

Quick as a flash, she replied, 'Hello, little f★★k!'

## Too Posh to Care

A yummy mummy at an elegant social gathering thrusts her wailing and very smelly baby at a nanny who works for another of the rich guests, ordering her to, 'Change it!'

'What into, madam,' came the reply, 'a bleedin' frog?'

## Keeping Mum

A Mafia Godfather finds out that his bookkeeper has screwed him out of 10 million bucks; his bookkeeper is deaf. It was considered an occupational benefit and the reason he got the job in the first place, since it was assumed that a deaf bookkeeper would not be able to hear anything that he'd ever have to testify about in court.

When the Godfather goes to shakedown the bookkeeper about his missing $10 million, he brings along his attorney, who knows sign language.

The Godfather asks the bookkeeper: 'Where is the 10 million bucks you embezzled from me?' The attorney, using sign language, asks the bookkeeper where the 10 million bucks is hidden.

The bookkeeper signs back: 'I don't know what you are talking about.'

The attorney tells the Godfather: 'He says he doesn't know what you're talking about.'

That's when the Godfather pulls out a 9 mm pistol, puts it to the bookkeeper's temple, cocks it, and says: 'Ask him again!'

The attorney signs to the underling: 'He'll kill you for sure if you don't tell him!'

The bookkeeper signs back: 'OK! You win! The money is in a brown briefcase, buried behind the shed in my cousin Enzo's backyard in Queens!'

The Godfather asks the attorney: 'Well, what'd he say?'

The attorney replies: 'He says you don't have the balls to pull the trigger.'

# Chapter Four

# The Revenge of Mother Nature

*'Revenge is often like biting a dog because the dog bit you.'*
*Austin O'Malley,*
*US physician and humorist (1858–1932)*

Have you noticed how we speak of Nature in the feminine
– describing her as Mother Nature? And how we give hur-
ricanes human names? When a natural disaster happens, we
tend to believe that the force of nature is deliberately turning against us.

In the same way, pet owners and film-makers alike are
renowned for their propensity to credit animals with human
characteristics and emotions. Is this just fanciful or could
animals really be capable of feeling emotion and perhaps
even wishing to exact revenge?

A recent study published in the *New Scientist* reports
that elephants appear to be attacking human settlements
as vengeance for years of abuse by people. Joyce Poole, the

research director at the Amboseli Elephant Research Project in Kenya, who co-authored a paper on elephant behaviour, says, 'They are certainly intelligent enough and have good enough memories to take revenge.'

Richard Lair, a researcher of Asian elephants at Thailand's National Elephant Institute, has seen the same problems arising in parts of India, particularly West Bengal, where villagers live in fear of attacks from bull elephants whom villagers claim come into the villages expressly to kill people.

In March 2005, two chimpanzees escaped from an animal sanctuary near Bakersfield, California and mauled a man. When questioned about the premeditated attack, Harvard anthropologist Richard Wrangham, one of the world's leading experts on primates, said, 'We know chimpanzees are capable of that sort of violence. In many parts of Africa, chimps have attacked and killed human babies. And they've done so as predators. There also have been a number of cases where chimps that were caged got out and the first thing they did was attack people. They are roughly 3–4 times stronger than humans, so the fight was no contest.'

Whether animals really do have it in for us, or whether the vast majority of incidences where animals appear to get even are accidental, is hard to judge. However, the following stories are a few examples of those occasions when Nature appears to be getting its own back on mankind.

# Malice Afterthought

Whether it's a cute and cuddly domestic pet or a fearsome wild predator, the following collection of stories seems to support the theory that animals may have the innate ability or the will to seek revenge …

## Cats Seek Revenge

Franny Syufy tells the story of how she had a grey-striped Manx cat called Bobby when she was a teenager. Her Texan stepfather, Bud, was a dog-lover but Bobby's powerful build and independent air soon convinced Bud that he could be the 'family dog'.

Franny's mum and Bud were keen outdoor people and often took Bobby with them on short hunting or fishing trips, which he loved.

One day, a three-week hunting trip in the wilds of Idaho was planned but they considered this trip too long to include Bobby. The cat watched them packing their hunting and fishing gear with growing anticipation. Imagine his disappointment when the pair petted him and said goodbye, safe in the knowledge that a neighbour was going to come in a feed Bobby and that he had a 'cat flap'.

On their return, they found carnage: the food dish overturned, poop in the middle of their bed, a dead rat in the toilet, a dead bird and feathers strewn around the living room.

Bobby was gone and never returned. As Franny says, 'I can't imagine a more eloquent and emphatic statement of anger and revenge, from one very ticked-off cat!'

## Elephants Never Forget

When travelling in Nepal, Michael Hodson, a barrister from Newcastle upon Tyne, was told the story of a cruel mahout (elephanteer) who once stubbed out his cigarette on a young elephant's tongue. Some years later, the same elephant picked up the man and crushed him to death.

## Parrot Squawks on Cheating Lover

In January 2006, Chris Taylor's parrot Ziggy began squawking 'Hiya, Gary' whenever his girlfriend Suzy Collins' mobile phone rang. The African Grey also made kiss noises each time it heard the name Gary on television or radio.

Chris, a computer programmer in Leeds, was simply amused until he snuggled up to his girlfriend Suzy on the sofa and Ziggy cried out in Suzy's voice, 'I love you, Gary.'

In the face of Ziggy's onslaught, Suzy broke down and confessed to having a four-month fling with a former colleague. She had met her lover in the flat while Ziggy looked on.

Her confession ended their two-year relationship.

Sadly, it was also the end of the road for Chris and Ziggy

– 'it was torture hearing him repeat that name Gary over and over,' Chris said and so Ziggy the whistle-blower was rehoused with a local parrot dealer.

## Hitchcock's 'The Birds'

The BBC reported the incident of a flock of crows who were attacking residents of Warwick. First, the crows targeted cars, scratching them and pulling off windscreen wipers. Then they reportedly moved on to humans. Colin Wilkinson, a conservation officer with the Royal Society for the Protection of Birds, suggested that people 'protect themselves by wearing hats' and not leave any food scraps around.

## Baaa-aaad Sheep

In 1992, Claire and Nick Marr, an English couple from London, were touring the UK on their Laverda motorcycle. As they crossed the remote Tomintoul Pass in the Scottish Highlands, a very large, shaggy Highland sheep, complete with horns, blocked their path. Nick slowed right down as he approached the sheep which, after a dismissive stare at the bike, started to trot away.

He then slowly opened the throttle to proceed when the insulted sheep had a change of heart and decided to head-butt the intruder. It reared up and struck the windshield but the force of the blow flicked the sheep over the heads of the driver and pillion rider.

However, the sheep still had the last laugh. Not only did the fright of flying through the air cause it to evacuate its bowels all over Claire, the pillion rider, but the damage it caused to the bike ran into thousands.

## Crossing The Fe-Line

A guy who lived in south-east London had a cat called Rebel. After the guy's father put the cat out on a particularly cold day, Rebel wreaked revenge by leaving a 'dirty' protest' in one of his slippers.

What most upset the father was not the fact that his slipper was full of cat poop but that Rebel had 'deliberately' pushed it down to the toe-end so that the father didn't notice until his foot was inside.

## Nutty Squirrel Nutkin

A fire chief in a Mississippi town was cruising on his Harley motorcycle in a quiet residential area when a squirrel ran out from under an oncoming car straight into his path. He thought impact was inevitable but, to his surprise, just before the wheel ran over the squirrel it rose on its hind legs and leapt in the air. It flew over his windscreen and hit him in the chest where it began to bite and claw him.

The surprised motorcyclist finally managed to grab the furious squirrel's tail with his gloved left hand and attempted to throw it clear. However, this was no ordinary squirrel.

Amazingly, the irate rodent managed to cling on to the finger of the glove and was swung around, landing squarely on the driver's back.

Rather than make his escape, the squirrel then proceeded to claw and tear at the man's T-shirt, causing him inadvertently to open the throttle of his Harley and pull a wheelie. He needed both hands on the handlebars to get the bike under control, which left the vengeful squirrel unimpeded. It ran up over the man's head and into the front of his motorcycle helmet and started hissing and screaming in his face. As the bike's engine maxed out – this was not the time to change gear – the man managed to grab the squirrel's protruding tail and, in desperation, he dragged the squirrel out of his helmet and flung it free … straight through the open window of a stationary police car.

The last thing the he saw in his rear-view mirrors was the police car with both doors flung open, one policeman on the grass verge and the other in the road pointing his gun in the car. A narrow escape.

# Oh No You Don't

As Scotland's best-loved bard, Robert Burns was wont to say, 'The best laid schemes o' mice an' men gang aft a-gley' (*To a Mouse*), which for those of you who don't understand

Scottish translates as, 'The best laid plans of mice and men go oft astray.' And Burns obviously knew a thing or two because, as we all know, nature can have a frustrating knack of thwarting man's enterprises.

## Biggest Banger Bid Beaten

Eighty cooks from Leipzig in Germany had created a 333-metre long sausage and looked set to steal the world record for grilling the world's longest sausage. However, the record attempt failed after gale force gusts put paid to any attempts to light the 294 grills laid end to end to cook the sausage. The first few grills were lit but strong winds scattered burning barbecue coals, causing a fire risk, so the world record bid had to be abandoned.

## Pretty Clever Polly

Thieves in El Salvador thought they had got away with the perfect robbery after a raid on a house in San Salvador. However, when the getaway car was stopped by police for a routine check, a parrot called Paquita, who was also taken in the raid, started squawking 'Robbery! Robbery!' Apparently, it was repeating what its owner said when she saw the robbers, reports *Las Ultimas Noticias*. The bird's chants were enough to raise police suspicions and they ran a check on the car and found the stolen goods. The gang was arrested and Paquita became a celebrity in El Salvador.

## Penguins Trick Zoo

At Bremerhaven Zoo in Bremen, the mating programme to help save endangered South American penguins was frustrated after it was discovered that three of the zoo's five penguin pairs were homosexual. Keepers at the zoo became suspicious and ordered DNA tests to be carried out on the penguins after they had been mating for years without producing any chicks.

The gay pairs had cunningly pretended to mate and one couple had even adopted a stone that they protected like an egg, so duping the mating programme experts.

Now the German zoo has imported four female penguins from Sweden in an effort to get the gay penguins to go straight. However, earlier experiments have shown great difficulties in separating homosexual animal couples so, in case the gay penguins resist the charms of the new girls, the zoo has also flown in two new male penguins to get the programme back on track.

## Canine Suicide Assassins

During World War II the Russians trained dogs with dummy mines strapped to their backs to run under tanks. The training went well but when the dogs were used on the battlefields with live mines, the training backfired stupendously. Instead of running under the German tanks, the dogs turned tail and ran back under the Russians' own tanks, because these were the tanks they recognised from training.

*Oops.*

## Massive Attack

You might remember the salvaged Mongolian fleet from Workplace Revenge, Chapter 3. It wasn't just the Chinese craftsmen who were out to get them. In 1281, the Mongolians were feeling pretty smug about the huge invasion fleet of 4,400 ships that they had amassed to invade Japan. Surely, victory was certain. However, a violent typhoon blew up unexpectedly and crushed the poor-quality ships, much to the relief of the Japanese.

# Turning the Tables

It's not always premeditated revenge that has the most effective results. Sometimes, in one of life's ironic little twists, unplanned and unforeseen outcomes can satisfy the most keen appetites for 'poetic justice', as we'll see from the next set of stories. The biter is bit, so to speak …

## Fathering Handbags

After years of terrorising the villagers around Lake Victoria, Uganda, Osama the man-eating crocodile was finally caught in 2005. But instead of killing the 16-foot monster the locals agreed to send one-tonne Osama to Uganda Crocs Ltd, purveyors of fine crocodile-skin handbags destined for the fashion shops of Italy and South Korea.

Now Osama, who is believed to have killed at least 83 people in the area, is being used as breeding stock – and his offspring are destined to become handbags.

## Man or Mouse?

When 81-year-old homeowner Luciano Mares of Fort Sumner, New Mexico caught a mouse in his house in January 2006, he didn't think of the consequences when he tried to dispose of it.

Mr Mares was burning leaves outside, so he threw the mouse into the fire. Unfortunately for Mr Mares, the burning mouse ran back into the house and fell just beneath a window. The Associated Press reported that flames spread throughout the house and all the contents of the home were destroyed.

## Fisherman's Tale

Glen Hopper, 43, from Queensland state's Sunshine Coast, told the Australian Associated Press of how a five-foot mackerel jumped into his boat, knocked him down and injured him – and then got away!

As Hopper was going 20 knots along the Mooloolah River and the 30-kilogram fish was speeding in the opposite direction, it was quite a collision. Hopper said, 'It felt like I'd just run into a brick wall. I remember it coming out the water and the next thing I knew, I'm in the back of the boat winded, trying to get my breath. It's fishy's revenge, I suppose.'

## Noise Pollution

We all hate having a nap disturbed by the sound of lawn-mowers or roadworks but a 14-and-a-half-foot crocodile called Brutus took matters into his own jaws when the sound of a chainsaw, which was being used to clear up debris left by a tropical storm that lashed northern Australia, got on his nerves.

Freddy Buckland was cutting up a tree that had fallen against a crocodile enclosure at the Corroboree Park Tavern, 50 miles east of Darwin, when Brutus apparently took exception to the chainsaw's noise and attacked.

The crocodile jumped out of the water and ran about 20 feet along the tree towards Buckland. He then grabbed the chainsaw in his jaws and shook and chewed the machine.

Neither Brutus nor Buckland were hurt in the attack but it took nearly two hours to get the chainsaw away from the irate crocodile.

Saltwater crocodiles have also been known to attack small powerboats, apparently because they don't like the noise of outboard motors.

## Putting His Foot in It

A serial burglar was caught after police tracked him down from a footprint he left in a pile of dog mess.

Timothy Groves, 29, left a print in poop left by dogs belonging to the Phillips family, whose home he burgled. A cast of the print was taken and, when Groves was arrested on suspicion of another burglary, his trainers were matched to the cast. He was sentenced to 20 months in jail. Incriminated by excrement, so to speak.

## Spider's Fiery Revenge on Nudist

In April 2006, reports appeared of a naked man who had suffered burns to one-fifth of his body after trying to set light to a spider at a nudist resort at the junction of the Wollondilly and Wingecarribee rivers in the New South Wales southern highlands.

The 56-year-old Sydney man mistook the unlucky arachnid – probably a harmless trapdoor spider – for a deadly funnel web spider and decided to kill it by pouring petrol down the spider's burrow and igniting it with a match, the NRMA CareFlight service said.

However, the fuel exploded and the naked man was left with burns to 18 per cent of his body, on the upper leg and buttocks. Resort staff tended to the man's wounds before he was flown by helicopter to a hospital in Sydney. The rescue chopper service believed that the man's lack of clothing probably contributed to the extent of his burns.

## Here Kitty Kitty

There are numerous reports of kids and adults teasing little kittens, but cats everywhere will be celebrating the following role-reversal tale from the United States.

While taking his morning shower, Ed heard his wife calling him from the kitchen to come and reset the waste disposal, which had ground to a halt. He protested but Deb, his wife, claimed she was scared of touching it.

Dripping water and buck naked, Ed came into the kitchen and leant into the cupboard under the sink to press the reset button. At that point, the new kitten, Buttons, saw the dangling 'toys' that Ed was unwittingly presenting and snagged them with her needle-sharp claws.

Ed reacted naturally enough by shrieking and leaping up – forgetting that he was in a cupboard. He was knocked out cold. When he finally came around, he couldn't help noticing that the paramedics standing over him were having a difficult job suppressing their giggles. His wife had told them the whole story.

## Dressed to Kill

Some tourists were driving in a car through the Australian bush when they hit a large male red kangaroo. The animal stood about six feet tall and the intrepid tourists decided it would make a very impressive photo opportunity. They propped the roo up and, to add that little bit of humour, one of the blokes lent it his jacket.

But of course it turned out the roo was only stunned, and he promptly hopped off into the distance complete with jacket, wallet and passport.

## Salad Dressing

Brian Boughton was a member of the Royal Society for the Protection of Birds, but for some time his home had been plagued by a flock of gulls nesting in the roof of his house. The final straw came when one of the gulls flew past a window and sprayed bird muck over his hair, jacket, curtains and wife Elizabeth's lunch. So Boughton shot it and hung its carcass in the orchard to deter other poop-happy gulls.

However, after a tip-off, RSPCA officers charged him with illegally killing a seagull. Dr Boughton was found guilty of killing a wild bird and given a one-year conditional discharge and ordered to pay £400 costs.

## Cold Snap

As farmer Gheorghe Popa, aged 52, from Galati in Romania watched his new 25-year-old wife hanging out the washing, nature took its course and he grew physically excited.

Unfortunately, he was so distracted that he dropped one of the heavy sacks of grain that he was moving to the barn, and it hit his erect penis, snapping vital tendons and ligaments.

The report quotes Dr Nicolae Bacalbasa as saying, 'It was a bizarre accident, and he was in a lot of pain. We have done what we can for him but he may never regain use of the organ again, at least for sexual purposes.'

*Mother Nature can be so cruel.*

# First Class

Two Cambridge undergraduates, David Jordan and James Cole, decided to post a live hamster in a card-backed envelope. They sent it 'as an act of revenge' to a man who had threatened Jordan after an argument several months earlier, Ely magistrates' court was told in January 2006.

However, the hamster – who would have been killed or seriously injured by the sorting machinery had she not been spotted by an eagle-eyed postman – had the last laugh. The pair were arrested after an anonymous tip-off and the court, which didn't believe the undergraduates' excuse that they had been drunk, fined Jordan £750 and Cole £500 and ordered each to pay costs of £100. Both are banned from keeping animals for ten years.

Happily, First Class, as the hamster has been named, was adopted by a nurse at a veterinary practice and is reported to be doing well.

# Getting it Wrong

Sometimes it is man who gets it wrong and sometimes it is nature that gets it wrong – either way, somebody or something pays the price ...

## Nature's Blooper

Allergy sufferers everywhere know that furry house-pets, particularly cats, can cause allergies and breathing difficulties in people. In a bizarre reversal of fortunes, scientists in Scotland have discovered that humans can trigger asthma attacks in cats. Apparently 1 in 200 cats suffers from feline asthma, and its symptoms – coughing, wheezing and shortness of breath – are aggravated by human dandruff, household dust, cigarette smoke and some types of human litter. Meanwhile ...

## Mankind's Slip-up

In medieval Europe, cats were feared and despised because they were believed to be in league with the devil. It was common for witch-burnings to be accompanied by mass cat-burnings. According to Barbara Holland in her book *Secrets of the Cat*, 'cats were burned, boiled, impaled, hanged, skinned alive, gutted alive, buried alive, dropped from towers, stoned, scalded and stabbed' during this anti-cat period.

Yet cats were to wreak a terrible revenge upon their medieval persecutors, albeit inadvertently. By ridding Europe of cats, its citizens had created the perfect environment for mice and rats – a cat's natural prey – to breed excessively. When the Crusaders returned on ships from the Holy Lands, they brought rats from Palestine that carried fleas infected with the bacteria that caused the Bubonic Plague or Black Death. With so few cats left, the pandemic wiped out a quarter of the European population between 1347 and 1352.

# The Last Laugh

## David and Goliath

A man walks into a bar one day and asks, 'Does anyone here own that Rottweiler outside?'

'Yeah, I do!' a biker says, standing up. 'What about it?'

'Well, I think my Chihuahua just killed him …'

'What are you talkin' about?' the biker says, disbelievingly. 'How could your little runt kill my Rottweiler?'

'Well, it seems he got stuck in your dog's throat!'

## Wild West Reprisals

A three-legged dog walks into a saloon in the Old West. He sidles up to the bar and says, 'I've come to settle the score. I'm looking for the man who shot my paw.'

## Bumper Sticker

'Heart Attacks – Nature's revenge for eating our animal friends.'

## Never Talk to the Parrot

Mrs Peterson phoned the repairman because her dishwasher had stopped working. He couldn't accommodate her with an 'after-hours' appointment and since she had to go to work, she told him, 'I'll leave the key under the mat. Fix the dishwasher, leave the bill on the counter, and I'll send you a cheque. By the way, I have a large Rottweiler inside named Killer; he won't bother you. I also have a parrot, and whatever you do, do not talk to the bird!'

Well, sure enough the dog, Killer, totally ignored the repairman, but the whole time he was there, the parrot cursed, yelled, screamed and drove him mad.

As he was ready to leave, he couldn't resist saying, 'You stupid bird, why don't you shut up!'

To which the bird replied, 'Killer, get him!!!'

## Two Angry Neighbours

Two neighbours had been fighting each other for nearly 40 years. Bob buys a Great Dane and teaches it to defecate in Bill's garden. For one whole year Bill ignores the dog.

So Bob then buys a cow and teaches it to defecate in Bill's garden. After about a year and a half of Bob's cow crapping in Bill's garden, being ignored all the while, a lorry pulls up in front of Bill's house.

Bob runs over and demands to know what's in the 18-wheeler.

'My new pet elephant,' Bill replies solemnly.

## Feeding the Crocodile

On a fine summer evening, a fruit farmer in Australia went out with a bucket to pick some of his finest fruit for dessert. As he approached his favourite trees, he heard giggling and laughing coming from beyond the bushes, in the direction of his farm's waterhole.

He crept nearer to investigate, only to be caught apparently red-handed by the group of teenage girls who were skinny-dipping in his pool.

'What you looking at, you dirty old man?' they taunted.

Smarting from the insinuation and thinking quickly, the farmer replied, 'I'm not looking at anything. I've just come down to the watering hole to feed my pet crocodile!'

*Touché.*

# Chapter Five

# Motoring Revenge

*'And where the offence is, let the great axe fall.'*
Macbeth, *William Shakespeare (1564–1616)*

Revenge is an emotion that has been present in man since time immemorial, but road rage and tales of motoring revenge have understandably only been around since the early 20th century.

It will probably come as no surprise that, according to research commissioned by Egg Motor Insurance, more than a third of people drive dangerously after becoming angry with other motorists. And a further two-thirds of drivers admit to being wound-up by other drivers' dangerous or aggressive behaviour. But most importantly, for the purposes of this book, a further 17 per cent actually admit to plotting revenge on careless or reckless motorists.

# Revenge is Sweet

Stress specialist Dr David Lewis, the psychologist who initially defined the 'road rage' term, has dubbed drivers' feelings of pent-up anger towards other motorists as 'revenge rage'.

'These drivers admit to being inwardly furious and brooding long and hard about motoring incidents, with one in six plotting revenge,' he said. '"Revenge rage" occurs when a driver becomes so caught up in their angry dreams of vengeance against the offending motorist that they are distracted from the essential task of driving safely.'

So what triggers revenge rage? According to those questioned, bad driving from others, especially those who recklessly overtake or cut in front of vehicles, is most likely (65 per cent) to cause obsessive thoughts of revenge. In fact, slightly more women than men (68 per cent to 60 per cent) fume furiously about such selfish driving.

And, in case you want to know who to watch out for, the survey also showed that those most susceptible to dreaming about vengeance or 'Road Rage' were low-mileage motorists (32 per cent), probably female (38 per cent women to 30 per cent men), and over 45. Oh dear – that sounds like me!

# Real Life Stories

As you will see in the next section, many of the stories that circulate about motoring revenge are urban legends that people have adopted and retold as their own. But the following collection of motoring mayhem and tales of retribution are all believed to be true. Sometimes, life is stranger than fiction.

# Getting a Mouthful

In 2004, Glaswegian pensioner John O'Hare, aged 73, and his 69-year-old wife May were spending a week touring Scotland in their camper van when they stopped off for the final night of their holiday in Helensburgh, on the Clyde.

During the night, a bungling thief tried to siphon diesel from their camper van but got a mouthful of raw sewage. The would-be raider missed the fuel tank in the dark and put a tube into the van's septic tank by mistake, according to a report in the *Daily Record* newspaper.

After sucking up the foul-smelling waste, the thief threw up on the spot and fled. In the morning, when he stepped out of the van, John found a puddle of vomit and an abandoned petrol container. He said, 'I hope the thief has learned from his experience and given up his evil ways.'

Also found at the scene was a pile of pound coins, which John believes may have been stolen from a vending machine earlier in the night. John and May donated the abandoned coins to Oxfam.

## Boxed In

A 24-year-old man was walking up to the supermarket when a guy in a BMW parked in the spot reserved for shopping trolleys. The man told him that it wasn't a parking space. The BMW driver simply sneered and went off to shop.

The snubbed man proceeded to gather up every trolley he could find in the car park and turned them on their sides, completely surrounding the car. One of the trolley collection boys even helped. They then sat on a bench in front of the store and waited. Soon the guy came out and, by all accounts, what he said would have made a sailor blush!

## Mistaken Identity

In the 1950s, a pompous consultant neurologist in the northeast of England was very proud of his sit-up-and-beg Bentley motorcar, which he loved to show off.

On one occasion, he was visiting some friends whose neighbour had the same sort of car – it was even the same colour. Tired of the visitor's bragging, the two sons crept from the house and, as people didn't bother to lock cars in those days, they were able to push the self-important neurologist's car to the end of the road. They then pushed the neighbour's car into the parking spot that the visiting neurologist's car had previously occupied (with me so far?).

When the time came for the neurologist to leave, he could not understand why his key wouldn't turn in the ignition. He became increasingly frustrated and upset until, finally, he saw his own car at the end of the street, gleaming in the lamplight.

## Who Cares

In Pickens County, South Carolina, the state troopers were involved in a high-speed chase with a man driving a Porsche. His driving was even more reckless than normal and the reason soon became clear.

The thief was a disgruntled employee who had stolen his ex-boss's car and, naturally, he didn't care at all if it got smashed up.

With its turbo-charged engine and travelling at speeds of over 100 mph, the Porsche was able to leave the state troopers squad cars way behind. But when the thief found himself in traffic, the odds were levelled. The result was almost inevitable – the thief slammed into a minivan in a queue of traffic and the car was totalled.

The disgruntled thief was led away in handcuffs and the ex-boss is left needing a new Porsche and a new employee.

## Hot Air

Albert Hall, a state representative in Montgomery, USA, took the law into his own hands when he became incensed after his car was blocked in by another vehicle. He decided to let the air out of the left front tyre of the offending car.

The *Decatur Daily* newspaper reports that Mr Hall, a house parking committee member, now regrets what he did – particularly since he later learned that the driver was the wife of another state representative, Allen Layson.

In his own defence, Hall said that he didn't let the tyre all the way down but 'I just wanted her to have to stop and put some air in her tyre and trouble her a little too.'

*Sounds like hot air to me!*

## Getting a Handle on Revenge

The only way that Susan could think to get back at her clock-watching, over-bearing boss was to ruin his day by wiping cat faeces that she had collected from the litter tray that morning on the inside of his driver's door handle. When he came to go home at the end of the day, he walked to his company car parked in the car park for senior staff and Susan watched as he got a nasty surprise as he went to open his car door.

He didn't have any wipes or tissues or anything with him to get the mess off his hand, so the time-slave was forced to relock the car and go back into the office building to wash his hands and to get some paper towels to clean his car door handle.

## Repair Man

An unscrupulous garage owner got his revenge on a customer who had patronised and been rude to him by carrying out unnecessary repairs to the man's car.

His simple but effective ploy was to put a pebble or a coin in the hub-cap of his customer's car each time he visited so that he could hear an irritating rattle when on the move.

Eventually, the authorities caught up with the garage owner who confessed that he had charged the man for endless amounts of unnecessary work in retaliation for his bad manners.

## Messy Come-uppance

This past summer a guy was going to the beach when he saw two young girls park a convertible in a handicapped space. He told them they couldn't park there. They ignored him. So he went back to his car and got a half-full bucket of popcorn leftover from the movie the night before, and poured that popcorn into their car. In no time, it was covered with seagulls eating popcorn and doing what birds do best.

## Taxi!

When Mick Marone worked in central London, he often had difficulty finding a cab late at night that was prepared to take him to his home in Kidbrook, a suburb in south London. He could hail a cab but more often than not, when the cab driver learnt of his destination, he would decline the fare and drive off.

Mick grew wise to this and devised a strategy to deal with uncooperative cabbies. When he hailed a cab, he would open the passenger rear-door as if to get in while telling the driver of his destination. If the driver said, 'Sorry mate, I won't go south of the water', he would walk off, leaving the rear passenger door open, obliging the cabbie to get out of his driver seat and walk around to close the door.

Petty but satisfying, Mick would say.

## Sense of Humour

A news story on a Chicago radio station reported a guy in California who got a speeding ticket that was sent to him through the post. He had been caught by one of the static 'cameras' that populate certain roads.

The camera took the picture of his speeding car and number plate. A letter was generated by a computer and was sent to him with the photograph of his speeding car together with the date and time of the offence. The letter informed him that he had to send in a fine of $40.

Apparently, the guy was so mad that he sent back the letter with a photograph of two $20 notes.

A week later, he got a letter back from the police. When he opened the envelope, inside was a photograph of a pair of handcuffs.

## Tables Turned

White Van Man (WVM) is the bane of British traffic police everywhere because of his propensity for reckless driving, speeding and law breaking. So, what better way to turn the tables and get revenge than for the police to use a white panel van to house hidden speed cameras?

The vans have been introduced in the Birmingham area and have two rear-facing digital cameras behind lift-up shutters that snap unwary drivers and fellow WVMs, then a computer database inside the van immediately verifies if the car is stolen or the tax has expired.

*Talk about sneaky!*

## Embarrassing Bonnet Mascot

After a long-running border dispute between two neighbours in California, Dirk decided to up the ante by plotting a revenge attack on his neighbour's prize possession – his Hummer car.

In this middle-class suburban neighbourhood, residents left their cars on the drive at night. Dirk crept out in the early hours of the morning armed with a large silver vibrator and some superglue. He then proceeded to adhere the sex-toy to the bonnet of his neighbour's car. Finally, he covered the vibrator in lubricant oil and returned to his home.

The next morning, Dirk watched as his neighbour left his house to leave for work. The guy did a double-take when he got to his beloved Hummer. With difficulty (the bonnet is extremely high on a Hummer), he climbed up to try and prise the article off the bonnet but his hands kept slipping off the lubricated super-glued vibrator.

By this time, a small number of early morning commuters who passed by on their route to the station had gathered and were watching his rather explicit efforts to remove the dildo.

Dirk watched the whole scene from his front window.

Much later, after the neighbour had managed to remove the vibrator from his car, but not before he had ruined the paintwork on the bonnet because the astringent used to unlock the adhesive also took off the paint, he accused Dirk of the vengeful act. Dirk pleaded ignorance and innocence and nothing could be proven. However, he was careful to garage his own car until the neighbour had moved – unsurprisingly, a 'for sale' sign had appeared in his garden not long after the vibrator incident.

## Cross Road Crossing

Meredith sat in the rush-hour traffic, inching her car forward in fits and starts. The traffic started to move and she followed the car in front. Unfortunately, her car was over the lines on a pelican crossing when the lights changed. She stayed where she was but it meant pedestrians had to walk around the front of her car to get to the other side. She felt rather embarrassed but was sure people would understand her predicament.

So she was completely shocked when she saw a well-dressed young woman reach into her bag and then heard a sharp noise as the woman passed the front of her car. She was also staring accusingly at Meredith during the whole incident.

Meredith leapt out of her car and sure enough, there was a scratch right down the front wing. The woman had reached the pavement and was disappearing in the crowds on the street. Meredith wanted to chase after her, but the lights had changed to green and cars behind were tooting.

She had no choice but to get back in the car and pay the price (literally) of inconveniencing a pedestrian.

## Smellorama

Nicole Green was not surprised when her ex-husband announced that he was going to remarry. However, she was surprised when she received an invitation to the forthcoming wedding.

She had behaved with quiet dignity throughout the divorce and everyone expected her to accept graciously and be pleased for Bob and his new wife.

Nicole duly accepted the invitation but she had a vengeful plan up her elegant sleeve. After the speeches, the best man and several others sloped off to decorate the happy couple's car, in which they were going to do a grand tour of the Continent for their three-week honeymoon. While the decorating party were occupied at the rear of the car, Nicole managed to hide a fresh fish on the heater system under the bonnet.

Weeks later, the news seeped back to her that it had taken the honeymooners days to find the source of the evil smell that threatened to ruin their grand tour. Apparently, the exclusive hotels in which they were supposed to stay were unimpressed by the car's unpleasant aroma.

To add to Nicole's satisfaction, the couple blamed the best man – thinking it was a wheeze that had gone too far. So Nicole got her revenge and also got off scot-free.

# Road Rage

**Nearly nine out of ten UK drivers report that they have been victims of road rage at least once, according to**

a 2003 *Max Power* magazine poll. And apparently, the British are the worst in the world for it. In a Gallup poll, of those who admitted committing road rage, three in five said that their victims 'deserved it'. Only 14 per cent showed any remorse for their actions and blamed a bad mood for what they'd done.

Road rage is not a new phenomenon but it does appear to be on the increase. It is hard to define road rage exactly but it covers any behaviour on the road ranging from gesticulating and verbally abusing another driver to cutting others up, driving too close and physical violence. Not surprisingly, the most common location for road rage is in town (54 per cent), followed by a major A road (17 per cent) or a motorway (15 per cent).

According to an article published by the Associated Press in June 2006, road rage is in fact the result of Intermittent Explosive Disorder (IED) which is an uncommon brain disorder characterised by explosive outbursts of behaviour that are disproportionate to the provocation. These findings were drawn from surveys of over 9,200 adults in the United States between 2001 and 2003.

It seems drivers all over the 'civilised' world are prone to 'losing it' when behind the wheel. Yet, rather refreshingly, a 2005 internet survey that rated Australian, Canadian, British and American drivers placed

Australian drivers as the most courteous and American drivers as the most aggressive. Thankfully, it also showed that figures for road rage were falling in all of those countries.

✂ ✂ ✂ ✂ ✂ ✂ ✂ ✂ ✂

# Motoring Urban Myths

The following apocryphal stories are told in various guises around the world. The fact that they are urban myths makes them no less funny and, who knows, perhaps they have their roots in a true incident of revenge.

## You've Been Dumped

A woman has saved for years to buy her husband who drives a cement mixer a Cadillac convertible for their anniversary.

When her husband comes home from work, the Cadillac is in the driveway and his wife is negotiating with the salesman. Seeing the flashy car, and seeing his wife talking with a strange man, the husband flies into a jealous rage and dumps his load of cement in the convertible.

## Car Park Counter Blow

In a crowded car park at a shopping centre, a woman is waiting patiently in her Mercedes while a man loads his shopping bags into the boot of his car. He finally gets into his car and reverses out, but before the woman can pull into the vacant space, two young girls in a little hatchback zip into the spot. Both girls get out, laughing, and start to walk away.

'Hey!' shouts the woman in the Mercedes, 'I've been waiting for that parking place.'

'Face it lady, we're younger and faster,' respond the teenagers.

At that instant, the woman puts her Mercedes in gear, pushes the accelerator to the floor, and crashes into the right rear-wing of the girl's car. Now, the girls are jumping up and down, shouting, 'You can't do that!'

The lady in the Mercedes says, 'Face it, I'm older and I have more insurance.'

*Variations on this general theme of the sassy youngster being hung by her – or in some cases – his own line by an older driver can be found on the internet. The most famous example of this tale of parking vengeance is from the bestselling novel* Fried Green Tomatoes, *which in 1991 was made into a film.*

## Bargain Hunter

A man in California saw an ad in the paper for an 'almost new' Porsche, in excellent condition – price $50. He was certain the printers had made a typographical error, but even at $5,000 it would have been a bargain, so he hurried to the address to look at the car.

A nice-looking woman appeared at the front door. Yes, she had placed the ad. The price was indeed $50. 'The car,' she said, 'is in the garage. Come and look at it.'

The fellow was overwhelmed. It was a beautiful Porsche and, as the ad promised, 'nearly new'. He asked if he could drive the car around the block. The woman said, 'Of course,' and went with him. The Porsche drove like a dream. The young man peeled off $50 and handed it over, somewhat sheepishly. The woman gave him the necessary papers and the car was his.

Finally, the new owner couldn't stand it any longer. He had to know why the woman would sell the Porsche at such a ridiculously low price. Her reply was simple: with a half-smile on her face, she said, 'My husband ran off with his secretary a few days ago and left a note instructing me to sell the car and the house, and send him the money.'

## Green-eyed Monster

A man goes to a car salesroom one day after inheriting a great deal of money. After looking around the dealership, he picks out the newest, fanciest, most expensive car he can. He pays cash up front and drives out of the dealership in the new car.

On his way home, he hears a rattling sound – something must be wrong. So he turns around and goes straight back to the dealer. The dealer is of course very sorry, and offers to either fix the car or let the man take a different one while they order a replacement. The man really wants the car, so he asks the man to fix it. Two hours later, the mechanics give the car back, saying they couldn't find a thing wrong with it. The man is a bit wary, but he drives home. Whatever the rattle is, it has stopped.

A day or so later, the rattle starts again. He takes it to the dealership, and they still can't find anything wrong with it. This continues for a number of weeks – sometimes the rattle even goes away on its own. After nearly two months of it, the dealer is very upset – he doesn't want to get a bad reputation. So he orders a replacement and exchanges it with the man for the malfunctioning car.

Then he orders the mechanics in the shop to completely dismantle the car to work out the problem. They begin taking the car apart, piece by piece, but they can't find anything – until they take apart the door. Inside, they find a piece of metal pipe, along with a note. Written on the note, in a scrawling, worker's hand is: 'So, you finally found the rattle, you rich son-of-a-bitch.'

## The Quiet Man

A lorry driver pulls up at a roadside café in the middle of the night for a spot of refreshment. Halfway through his dinner, three wild-looking motorcyclists roar up – bearded, leather-jacketed, filthy – with swastikas adorning their chests and helmets.

For no reason at all they select the lorry driver as a target. One pours pepper over his head, another steals his dessert, the third deliberately upsets his cup of tea. The lorry driver doesn't say a word – he simply gets up, pays his bill, and leaves.

'That bozo isn't much of a fighter,' sneers one of the bullies. The man behind the counter, peering out into the night, adds, 'He doesn't seem to be much of a driver either. He just ran his lorry right over three motorcycles.'

*(All these motoring myths and more can be found at snopes.com.)*

# The Last Laugh

## Insurance Revenge

Two cab drivers met. 'Hey,' asked one, 'why did you paint one side of your cab red and the other side blue?'

'Well,' the other responded, 'when I get into an accident, you should see how all the witnesses contradict each other.'

## Catch Me if You Can

A domineering husband is driving his wife home after a party. Suddenly, a policeman pulls his car over and tells the man that he was going 50 mph in a 30 mph zone.

'I was only going 30!' the husband protests.

'Not according to my radar,' the officer replies.

'Yes, I was!' the man shouts back.

'No you weren't!' the policeman says, starting to get annoyed. With that, the man's wife leans towards the window and says,

'Officer, I should warn you not to argue with my husband when he's been drinking.'

## People in Glasshouses

At a computer Expo (COMDEX) Bill Gates reportedly compared the computer industry with the auto industry and stated, 'If GM had kept up with technology like the computer industry has, we would all be driving $25 cars that go 1,000 miles per gallon.' Recently General Motors addressed this comment by releasing the statement: 'Yeah, but would you want your car to crash twice a day?'

# Chapter Six

# Sporting Revenge

*'One good act of vengeance deserves another.'*
John Jefferson, author

In most big sports today, gamesmanship and mild dirty tricks are an accepted – almost expected – tactic. No one bats an eyelid when a tennis player calls a serve out that he or she clearly sees is in. Similarly, cricketers stay at the stumps when they know they are out and claim catches that never hit the bat, while front-row rugby forwards drop the scrum near the posts in the hope of winning their side a penalty.

In fact, no sport is free of these attempts to steal one over on the opposition or match officials – even in the noble sport of golf, players have been known to give themselves a favourable drop or change their scorecards.

It is this feeling that the opposition is not playing fair or that they are getting away with it that can lead to feelings of resentment on the playing field and, in turn, this bitterness can lead to acts of retaliation or revenge. In physical sports such as rugby, football, ice hockey etc, these mounting frustrations and stewing resentments are often settled there and then when tempers fly and a punch-up ensues. But in other sports, players take their time to think up ways of getting back at opponents who have behaved badly in their eyes. And guess what, sportsmen and women are actively seeking revenge on opponents or game officials – are we surprised? I guess not.

# Most Unsporting!

The desire for revenge in the sporting arena can lead to conduct unbecoming. The following collection of avengers surely deserve the yellow card at the very least but, what the ref doesn't see …

## Nifty Parking

While on a rugby tour of Italy in 1980, a team from England's north-east played a hard match against a home team. However, the visitors felt that the Italian referee was unfairly biased in favour of the home team.

After the match, the English team players went out drinking in the town, still smarting from the defeat and the unfair treatment from the official. Whilst in a bar, they saw the ref arrive in town in his little Fiat 500 car which he parked before heading off to a restaurant.

It only took a few more drinks to be consumed before the burly UK rugby players decided to seek retribution for the injustice. The team gathered around the tiny car and physically lifted it from its parking spot and placed it in the doorway of a large shop. It was in full view but there was no room in front or behind the car for the referee to get out of his 'new' parking space.

## Transfer Revenge

When Romanian defender Marius Cioara was bought for a transfer fee of 15 kilograms of pork sausages, the insult was so great that he decided to spite the club and turn his hand to farming in Spain instead of playing 'the beautiful game'.

A spokesman for his new fourth division team, Regal Hornia, told the media that they had given up the team's sausage allowance for a week to secure Cioara, but they had thought it was a price worth paying.

However, the sausage taunts were too much for the player and he packed his kit the day after details of the deal were leaked to the media.

The club are now demanding a refund from second division UT Arad, who sold the defender for sausages.

## Rio's Wind-ups

England and premier-league footballer Gary Neville played a prank on fellow player Rio Ferdinand when he put yogurt all over his brand new car. Not only did Ferdinand vow to get even, he decided to televise his revenge.

His reprisal on Neville was the first of a televised series of six 'wind-ups' played on England football stars (*Ferdinand's World Cup Wind-Ups*) but with Neville, of course, it was personal. Knowing that there are two things in particular that get under Gary Neville's skin – namely Scousers and policemen – Ferdinand set the trap.

As Neville drove his shiny black SUV into an underground car park, a police car pulled up alongside and a uniformed Merseyside bobby got out. He gently wound up Neville, reeling off a list of driving offences in a mocking fashion. And Neville obviously got increasingly irritated. The fake policeman then told Neville that he must accompany him to the station and get six points on his licence or … he could pose for a photo with him, and he'd let him off.

Despite the temptation, Neville's pride wouldn't let him have his photo taken with the cheeky Scouse copper – and through gritted teeth he said, 'Just give me the six points. I'm not negotiable.'

At which point, he was let in on the prank.

*Watch your back, I say, Ferdinand! He wasn't too impressed.*

## Jock's Strops

A group of American high school jocks had made the lives of other pupils who didn't fit 'the norm' an absolute misery. When they spray-painted the drive of one of their 'geek' victims, it was time for the bullied to unite.

At the next home football match, the avenging horde started chanting the team's latest scorelines – none of which were very impressive. The jocks had red-faces and the nerds gained some new-found respect for being thrown out of the game.

## Red Faced

A Brazilian football referee is facing divorce proceedings after pulling a pair of red lacy knickers out of his pocket instead of a red card during a match, according to a report in *Terra*.

It was during an amateur match that referee Carlos Jose Figueira Ferro attempted to use the knickers to send off footballer Paulo Coise. He was so embarrassed by the discovery that he ended the match 20 minutes early. He claims that he has no idea how the knickers ended up in his pocket but this explanation didn't satisfy his wife who reportedly started divorce proceedings after the match.

Rumour has it that this is a case of an aggrieved player avenging himself against a match official.

# Sporting Revenge

## Soccer Aid

A friendly rivalry developed between the two teams, England vs Rest of the World, during the lead-up to the recent UNICEF fund-raiser, Soccer Aid.

To wind up the opposition, the Rest of the World team cut the toes out of the England team's white soccer socks. The England team were not amused and decided to retaliate.

Their plan was to water bomb the opposition in their changing rooms. However, the revenge plan was thwarted for two reasons. Firstly, the Rest of the World team had cunningly left an aide guarding the door to their locker room and secondly, as fellow England teammate Bradley Walsh pointed out, although the raiders had sneakily masked their identity by wearing the mutilated socks over their heads, they were still wearing their kit – with their names across the back!

## Check Mates?

Somehow you half-expect sportsmen on the field to resort to fisticuffs to sort out their differences but when it is a chess grandmaster throwing the punches, it comes as something of a surprise. Read on ...

In June 2006, the Chess Olympiad was held in Turin. This is an event that is held every two years between 150 international teams and it brings together the world's best chess players.

When a member of the British team, Danny Gormally, saw Levon Aronian, the leading light of the Armenian team, dancing with 19-year-old Australian grandmaster Arianne Caoili, known as the Anna Kournikova of the chess world, and also the object of Mr Gormally's attentions (they had been in an email relationship and seen together in London) at a post-event party, he saw red. He went on to the dance floor and punched and shoved Mr Aronian, who ended up on the floor.

The next day, the England captain apologised to the Armenian team for the unseemly events of the previous night. However, when Gormally went out for a coffee with friends, he was attacked by a group of young Armenian players bent on revenge for their star player. Where will it all end?

Just to put things in perspective, in Armenia, where chess is the national sport, 23-year-old Aronian is almost worshipped by his adoring public and, according to chess experts, he is treated like David Beckham over there. Perhaps he and Caoili are destined to be the Posh and Becks of the chess world?

## Surf's Up

On a surf trip, a surfer drew various sexual organs on the bottom of his friend's surfboard with a marker pen. The friend took revenge by wiping it off with acetone, and a cloth. Not just any cloth though, he stole the culprit's boxer shorts, and once finished left them under the poor guy's pillow! He had a crunching headache the next morning.

Re-revenge was then taken by stealing a film photo camera belonging to the original victim, and taking a five-shot sequence of an Indonesian stray dog having his teeth brushed, before returning both the camera and the tooth-brush to the unsuspecting man. On his return home after the surf trip, he was almost sick when the film was devel-oped and he realised he'd been cleaning his teeth with the offending toothbrush! He is still plotting a reply.

# Sour Grapes

Sometimes being beaten by a bitter rival can leave a very bad taste in a sportsperson's mouth – or, it seems, in the col-lective mouth of a sporting nation. And that can lead to an overwhelming desire for revenge by the fans.

## Vote Hijacking

When London mayor, Ken Livingstone, asked people to post suggestions for the name of the bridge at the new Wembley Stadium on the London Development Agency website, he was not expecting the name Dietmar Hamann to be high on the list.

However, German fans took the opportunity to nominate Hamann who scored the last goal at the old stadium, as a way of paying back the English for beating them in the 1966 World Cup finals at Wembley.

German newspapers urged readers to visit the site to cast their votes for Hamann, but, not to be outdone in the revenge stakes, the Australians were also reportedly trying the same stunt, by circulating an email calling on Aussies to vote for the bridge to be named after former rugby captain, John Eales.

For those who like to see right triumph and plans of revenge thwarted ... the actual winner was Billy, the white horse who, together with his rider PC George Scorey, restored order and calmed the crowds after a 100,000-strong pitch invasion during Wembley's first FA Cup final in 1923 between Bolton Wanderers and West Ham.

## Make My Day

After Jonny Wilkinson's late drop goal gave England the Rugby World Cup against their Australian rivals in the 2003 final, the Australian press planned to get their own back.

A feature entitled 'Rugby and revenge' appeared in the *Sydney Morning Herald* in April 2003 urging Australian readers to vote for Tim Henman instead of Wilkinson in the BBC's Sports Personality of the Year award.

The editorial said, 'There's nothing quite as satisfying as the taste of sour grapes washed down with a big glass of sweet revenge, especially when Jonny Wilkinson is involved.' It adds, 'In the interests of bad sportsmanship, readers should go to www.bbc.co.uk and click on the sports section. Vote Tim Henman and make Jonny's day.'

Despite the Australian's best efforts, Wilkinson was crowned Sports Personality of the Year in December 2003.

## Out of Line

Arsenal Football Club supporters were not best pleased when one of the match officials for the 2006 Champions League finals, Drammens Tidende, was pictured in his local paper wearing an opposition (Barcelona) shirt a few days ahead of the match.

Ole Hermann Borgan, the Norwegian referee, explained that it had been 'insensitive and stupid' to agree to be photographed in the shirt.

UEFA, the governing body of European football, agreed and dropped him from the match, reasoning that the Norwegian's gaffe cast doubt on his impartiality.

## A Chilling Tale …

In the Euro 2004 quarter-final between England and Portugal, with the score at 1-1, Urs Meier, the Swiss referee disallowed a goal by Sol Campbell in the 89th minute due to a foul by John Terry on the Portuguese goalkeeper.

The match ended in a draw, and Portugal proceeded to the next stage following a penalty shoot-out and reached the final (where it lost to Greece). Meier's decision was highly controversial and most English football fans saw no reason to disallow the goal, even though he received backing from UEFA for his decision.

In retaliation, the British tabloid press published Herr Meier's personal details and urged the public to vent their spleens. Meier received death threats, more than 16,000 abusive emails and even had an English flag placed at his home. Things were so bad that he was placed under police protection.

Despite the threats, Meier continued to receive FIFA appointments and to referee in the Swiss top division until he reached the mandatory retirement age for each.

✂ ✂ ✂ ✂ ✂ ✂ ✂ ✂ ✂

# Salutary Warning

**A 46-year-old retired army man, Christophe Fauviau, was sentenced to eight years in prison after the French court found him guilty of spiking the drinks of nearly 30 of his children's tennis rivals so that they would falter on the court, and causing the accidental death of one of his son's opponents when the player fell asleep at the wheel of his car and crashed.**

He said in court, 'I couldn't handle this sport anymore, seeing my kids play. Somehow, I lost all sense
of reason.'

✂ ✂ ✂ ✂ ✂ ✂ ✂ ✂ ✂

# One in the Eye for You

As Frank Sinatra is famously quoted as saying, 'the best
revenge is massive success'. The following sportsmen obviously hold this sentiment close to their hearts.

## Keep the Faith

As part of his editorial argument on a US sports website,
Rick Reilly urged voters to make USC quarterback Matt
Leinart Sportsman of the Year 2005 'if only to prove to every
cross-eyed, fat and bullied kid that someday, revenge can be
theirs.' Apparently that description fitted Leinart until he
was 14.

## Lapping it Up

After Fernando Alonso broke Michael Schumacher's title-
winning streak in 2005 by taking the world title, there were
many pundits and Formula 1 fans who spoke of the end of
an era and retirement for the German ace.

However, in April 2006, Michael Schumacher managed

to pull a fast one over Alonso at the San Marino track to win revenge for Ferrari and to silence his critics.

The race victory saw Schumacher break the late Ayrton Senna's record for pole positions, and increased his own record for victories (to 85) so his revenge was doubly sweet.

# Nerds FC

In Denmark, a clever TV producer jumped on the reality TV show bandwagon and came up with the idea for a new show. The plan was to find 16 self-confessed nerds who had never touched a football and who were more comfortable in front of a PC than a goal, to spend three months training them with a professional coach, and then to conclude the whole humiliating experience by pitting them against a professional team in a grand finale.

Audiences expected to enjoy poking fun at the inept nerds (who were truly awful at football) but unexpectedly, the team not only loved the 'bonding' experience of a team sport but, against all the odds, they were able to score a goal in the Big Match.

For one player, the sweet revenge of success was made all the more sweet by the fact that he couldn't join the rest of the original cast for series two, because his new-found fame had seen him elected to the Danish Parliament.

The show has spawned spin-off versions across Europe and even as far as Australia where the show is called *Nerds FC*.

## Turning the Other Cheek

In 1974, the reputation of Celtic's star player, Jimmy 'Jinky' Johnstone, preceded him so that when his team met Atletico Madrid, he was targeted for particularly rough treatment by the opposition.

In fact, three Atletico players were sent off for kicking Johnstone and he was assaulted at the end of the match – ending up with spit in his hair and bruises everywhere. Yet, each time he was targeted by an opposition player, Jinky would get up and carry on with the game.

His revenge was to make the opposition look small. That said, it's rumoured that his teammates did not share his ability to turn the other cheek, and they exacted their revenge for Johnstone in the tunnel.

# The Last Laugh

## Tough Golf Hole

A man and his wife are out golfing one day when they come up to the hardest hole on the course; it goes downhill and you can't quite see where your drive goes. So they tee off and walk down the hill and, there's the man's ball – right in front of a big barn.

The wife says, 'If we open both barn doors, you should have a clear shot to the green.'

The man agrees, and so they open both of the doors. He hits his ball and it makes it through the first set of doors but hits the far wall and comes ricocheting back – hitting his wife on the head and killing her.

A few months pass and he is out golfing again with his buddies. They come up to the same hole and, wouldn't you know it, the man's ball is right behind the barn again. One of his golf buddies says, 'Perhaps if we open both barn doors, you will have a clear shot to the green.'

The man replies, 'Nah, last time I tried that I got a 7.'

## Pricked Balloon

Egotistical Harry was always reminding people that he played semi-pro baseball.

'I had all sorts of tricks to confuse the opposition,' he told his friends. 'I was the James Bond type of player.'

'Batted .007,' his wife added.

## Winners and Losers

One day, an American was touring Spain. After his day's sight-seeing, he stopped at a local restaurant. While sipping his wine, he noticed a sizzling, scrumptious-looking platter being served at the next table. Not only did it look good, the smell was wonderful. He asked the waiter, 'What is that you just served?'

The waiter replied, ' Ah señor, you have excellent taste! Those are bull's balls from the bullfight this morning. A delicacy!'

# Sporting Revenge

The American, though momentarily daunted when he learned the origin of the dish, said, 'What the hell, I'm on vacation! Bring me an order!'

The waiter replied, 'I am so sorry, señor. There is only one serving a day since there is only one bullfight each morning. If you come early tomorrow and place your order, we will be sure to serve you this delicacy!'

The next morning, the American returned, placed his order and was served the one and only special delicacy of the day. After a few bites, and inspecting the contents of his platter, he called to the waiter and said, 'These are much, much smaller than the ones I saw you serve yesterday!'

The waiter promptly replied, 'Si señor! Sometimes the bull wins!'

# Chapter Seven

# Things Bite Back

*'Getting even is one reason for writing.'*
*William Gass,*
*US writer and author (1924–)*

'Revenge Effects' is a new term that was coined in the 1990s by the American writer and academic Edward Tenner to describe the unsettling way in which unintended consequences often flow from the new technologies and social changes that mankind engineers.

He observed in a piece entitled 'Voice Mail and Fire Ants', published in the *New York Times* on 26 July 1991, 'The world seems to be getting even with mankind, twisting our cleverness against us. Or we may be unconsciously twisting it ourselves. This is not a new phenomenon, but technology has magnified it. Wherever we look we face unintended consequences of mechanical, chemical, medical, social and financial ingenuity. They are revenge effects, and they are less the malignant ironies of a spiteful world than the results of a lack of human foresight.'

This chapter will look at just two of the areas fraught with 'revenge effects,' namely the mechanical and financial sectors.

# Go Gadget

Modern 'revenge effects' include the antibiotics that have led to new and more virulent bacteria, high-tech ski-boots to reduce ankle injuries that are causing knee injuries, low-tar cigarettes that induce people to smoke more ... and the list goes on. Here are a few examples of mechanical and technological products that have turned around and bitten us on the bum.

## Cryogenics Cock-up

In March 2006, the freezer in which Raymond Martinot and his wife Monique, founding members of the cryonics movement, were stored malfunctioned. The pair were frozen after death in the hope that modern science would be able to resurrect them at some point in the future.

Ironically, their son Remy has now had to have them cremated, after the freezer at their chateau in the Loire valley, France, suffered a technical fault, leaving them to defrost, according to a report in the *Guardian* newspaper.

Remy commented: 'I feel bitter that I could not respect my father's last wishes. Maybe the future would have shown that my father was right and that he was a pioneer.'

## Lost in Translation

Toyota, the Japanese car giant, were somewhat surprised when their highly successful model, the MR2, failed to live up to sales expectations in France, until it dawned on a Francophile that MR2 in French is pronounced 'Em-Err-Deux' which, when said quickly sounds like 'merde'.

*And deux is pronounced ... Duh!*

## Scenic Route

In May 2006, it took an ambulance nearly two hours to take an injured girl to hospital after it was misdirected to the scene of an accident by its satellite navigation system.

Chloe Banks, aged ten, was left lying by the roadside for almost an hour waiting for the ambulance after being injured in a car crash. Fortunately, her injuries were not serious.

There have been other reported cases of the 'revenge effects' of satellite navigation systems such as the woman who was sent from the north of England to Devon via Ireland.

The satnav 'revenge effect' is providing one village with hours of entertainment – and a few bob to boot. Since a road closure, drivers have been following the directions from their navigation aids only to find that the recommended route goes through a ford in the Wiltshire village of Luckington. Since the road closure, an average of one or two motorists a day have been towed out of the ford after failing to notice or ignoring warning signs about deep water. Some canny farmers have been charging £25 to pull the unfortunate drivers out with their tractors.

More seriously, UK motorists were sent to the edge of a 100ft drop on an unclassified road in North Yorkshire in April 2006 – 'revenge effects' gone mad!

# Communications Revenge

Undoubtedly, the latest advances in mobile technology have given us greater access to friends, family and business contacts. Computer programs such as target-specific databases and mail merge mean that even the smallest business can now send advertising and marketing material to potential clients. Yet, as we all know, the more sophisticated our world becomes, the greater the opportunity for 'revenge effects'.

## Wrong Button
The marketing assistant of an on-line sales company caused his company untold hassle from disgruntled customers and

opportunistic opposition when he sent their e-newsletter out to the database of clients but failed to use the bcc option, using the cc option instead, thus allowing other companies and customers to see the email addresses of all their clients.

*Whoops.*

## Wrong Number

The regional director of a charity sent a saucy text message to her husband Nick, saying, 'Knocking off early. I'll be waiting for you in bed.' Unfortunately, her boss was also called Nick and he was listed next to the husband in her mobile phone address book. It was the boss who received the invitation (and admission of leaving work early!).

## Accidental Dialling

The problem with ever-smaller mobile phones is that it's harder and harder to make sure they don't accidentally call someone while jostling in your handbag or pocket.

This is exactly the situation that *Sunday Times* magazine columnist, Christa D'Souza, found herself in when her nanny accidentally sat on her mobile in the car and speed dialled the writer, who then overheard the flirtatious conversation between the nanny and the journalist's teenage step-son – a conversation that she would have preferred not to have been privy to, and more than a bit embarrassing for the nanny.

## Snail Mail

Not all glitches are with new technology. A letter that was posted in London to a George Green in March 1950 by a woman called Gwen, inviting him to lunch has been delivered – 56 years too late.

According to the *Sun* newspaper, she writes: 'George, will meet at Monty's next weekend. Is 2 pm acceptable? Love Gwen.'

When the letter arrived at Cambridge University's Trinity College, staff were so intrigued that they had to open it.

*Did the Royal Mail ruin a beautiful romance? Or did the couple pick up the phone and rearrange the date? We'll never know.*

## Telemarketers

With the advent of detailed customer databases, our personal contact details have become public property – hence telemarketers. But some people are fighting back and gaining their revenge on the cold-callers who always ring at the most inconvenient times.

Neil Geitz explains on the internet his tips for getting the telemarketers to hang up on you. His favourite is to ask them if he can call them back. They invariably respond that they only have outgoing lines, to which he replies, 'But you have a phone at home, don't you? And you're calling me at home, right? So give me your home phone number and I'll call you.' He says, 'It's odd but they always hang up.'

He also gives an invaluable insider tip: apparently, a former telemarketer told him that they 'rate' their phone numbers ranging from 'sucker, will buy anything' to 'troublesome time-wasters'. His recommendation is that you get yourself placed on the latter list as soon as possible. He reasons, 'The various telemarketing companies trade (sell) this information to each other, and so "playing the waiting game" will help to get you placed on *their* "do not call" list.'

## Junk Mail

Here are two ways that people have found to get even with those who send unsolicited mail.

Matthew Roberts, a secretary at a pharmaceutical company in England keeps the pre-paid envelopes that come in advertisement packets on his desk together with a blank sheet of envelope labels. When he needs to send a letter or bill, he overlays the original mailing address on the pre-paid envelope with a blank sticker so he can write the address of his choice.

This tactic has become less effective in recent years, as more response envelopes come with a barcode that directs the envelope to a specific location.

Stella from the US tells on the internet of how she resorted to another method of getting even with the 'junk mail' companies. She collects all the 'junk mail' that arrives throughout the week, eg credit card and loan offers, sweepstake entries, and she puts the entire contents, including the envelopes in which it came (having carefully removed all traces of her name/address) in the return prepaid envelope and sends it right back.

Stella says, 'Now they're getting their own junk mail right back, and it doesn't cost me a penny! Now ain't *that* some payback?!'

# Financial Revenge

Revenge can be sweet in many different ways but hitting someone in the wallet is hugely satisfying to anyone hell-bent on revenge. Hitting big business is just an extension of this principle and 'it cost me dear' should be etched on the memories of all these victims of financial reprisals.

## Erotic Euros

It's not often that a member of the general public manages to get even with financial institutions but in March 2006 shopkeepers in Germany fell prey to a master forger and, apparently, master of revenge. Fake euros bearing pictures of naked men and women have been accepted by the good burghers of Cologne.

The notes are also printed with the word 'Eros', Greek god of love, rather than 'euros' and are circulating in high denominations of 300, 600 and 1,000.

A customer in a newsagent in Cologne bought some cigarettes with a large denomination note and left the store with €534 (£368) in real change.

*But will the banks help out the duped shopkeepers? I think not.*

## Faint Praise

Below is an actual letter (or so the circulating email claims) that was sent to a bank by a 96-year-old woman. The bank manager – not normally known for their sense of humour – is said to have thought it amusing enough to send it to the *New York Times*. It's lengthy, but well worth the read:

To whom it may concern:

I am writing to thank you for bouncing my check with which I endeavoured to pay my plumber last month. By my calculations, three nanoseconds must have elapsed between his depositing the check and the arrival in my account of the funds needed to honour it. I refer, of course, to the automatic monthly transfer of funds from my modest savings account, an arrangement which, I admit, has been in place for only 31 years.

You are to be commended for seizing that brief window of opportunity, and also for debiting my account

$30 by way of penalty for the inconvenience caused to your bank.

My thankfulness springs from the manner in which this incident has caused me to rethink my errant financial ways. I noticed that whereas I personally attend to your telephone calls and letters, when I try to contact you, I am confronted by the impersonal, overcharging, pre-recorded, faceless entity, which your bank has recently become.

From now on, I, like you, choose only to deal with a flesh-and-blood person. My mortgage and loan repayments will therefore and hereafter no longer be automatic, but will arrive at your bank, by check, addressed personally and confidentially to an employee at your bank whom you must nominate. Be aware that it is an offence under The Postal Act for any other person to open such an envelope.

Please find attached an Application Contact Status form, which I require your chosen employee to complete. I am sorry it runs to eight pages, but in order that I know as much about him or her as your bank knows about me, there is no alternative. Please note that all copies of his or her medical history must be countersigned by a Public Notary, and the mandatory details of his/her financial situation (income, debts, assets and liabilities) must be accompanied by documented proof. In due course, I will issue your employee with a PIN number, which he/she must quote in dealings with me. I regret that it cannot be shorter than 28 digits but, again,

# Revenge is Sweet

I have modelled it on the number of button presses required of me to access my account balance on your phone bank service. As they say, imitation is the sincerest form of flattery.

Please allow me to level the playing field even further. When you call me, you will now have a menu of options on my new voice mail system to choose from. Please press the buttons as follows:

1. To make an appointment to see me.

2. To query a missing payment.

3. To transfer the call to my living room in case I am there.

4. To transfer the call to my bedroom in case I am sleeping.

5. To transfer the call to my toilet in case I am attending to nature.

6. To transfer the call to my mobile phone if I am not at home.

7. To leave a message on my computer, a password to access my computer is required. Password will be communicated to you at a later date to the Authorized Contact.

8. To return to the main menu and to listen to options 1 through 7.

9. To make a general complaint or inquiry. The contact will then be put on hold, pending the attention of my automated answering service. While this may, on occasion, involve a lengthy wait, uplifting music will play for the duration of the call.

Regrettably, but again following your example, I must also levy an establishment fee of $50 to cover the setting up of this new arrangement. Please credit my account after each occasion.

May I wish you a happy, if ever so slightly less prosperous, New Year.

Your Humble Client.

*Remember, allegedly, a 96-year-old woman penned this letter. Whatever. It feels good to hear of someone getting even with faceless financial institutions.*

## On the Ball

Angela Kennedy from Wilmslow, Cheshire was so fed up at being left behind while her husband and son went to football matches that she decided to entertain herself by betting on the beautiful game. She studied football statistics and placed an accumulator bet on nine footballing eventualities and, lo and behold, she won nearly a quarter of a million pounds. Each of her hunches proved correct and so the bookmakers converted her initial stake of £2,000 into £242,391.

*Do you think the boys have had a change of heart and take her with them to matches now?*

## Wedding Hell

A plot to ruin one couple's happy day was foiled by the good services of two local police officers.

It seems that someone who was jealous of the couple's business success (they were newcomers to the area) sought revenge by sending a cancellation letter to the registrar calling off the wedding. Chris Walters and his wife-to-be turned up at the register office in Rhyl on a Saturday afternoon, only to discover that the building was locked and the registrar had gone home.

Two police officers came to the couple's aid – they tracked down the missing registrar and rushed her back to conduct the ceremony, which took place only 30 minutes late in the end.

The day turned out to be as wonderful as they could have hoped, no thanks to the hoaxer who let jealousy of a couple's business success lead to a rotten act of revenge.

# Paying the Price

The stories included in this book focus on the more humorous ways in which people seek to gain revenge and it is hoped that you find it amusing to hear of the inventive, witty and light-hearted ways in which some people choose to get even with others. However, sounding a cautionary note here, it's worth bearing in mind that seeking revenge can be a very costly business.

## Internet Sex Video

Ferdinand Holzl of Marburg in Germany sought revenge on his ex-lover by releasing a sex video of her on to the internet. Not content with that, he also posted her name, address and contact details.

However, the courts caught up with him and he was fined £24,000 and given an 18-month suspended sentence after being found guilty of criminal insult and trafficking in pornography.

## Too Hasty

A court in Buenos Aires ordered a man to pay £10,000 to his ex-wife as compensation for 'hurting her morals'. The couple were divorcing but the man moved in with his new girlfriend before the divorce was finalised, reports newspaper *Clarin*.

The judge concluded that couples should remain faithful until the marriage is legally dissolved and this guy was guilty of jumping the gun. Or, as the judge put it, 'This man acted with disregard for his wife's dignity. He caused her pain.'

## Laugh Like a Hyena

The defenceless animals whose cause is championed by the likes of the Environmental Liberation Front and Animal Liberation Front would be laughing now (metaphorically speaking) if they knew that the 10,000 or so disruptive incidents pulled off in their name since 1986 have cost the US more than $100 million in damage.

And, if you add to that the millions of dollars that have been spent on legal fees, the increased costs of security for animal testing centres and the financial implication of harassment for workers at circuses, zoos etc, then it could be said that the animals are having the last laugh.

## Tit for Tat

Two American businessmen ended up in court after one man created lewd images of the other and posted them on the internet using his rival's business name in the website address.

Richard Boucher, owner of Boucher's Furniture Store in Milford, and Nick D'Augustine, owner of Oak Furniture Store in nearby Amherst, had a history of business bickering.

After D'Augustine advertised wholesale prices on items

similar to those sold by Boucher, Boucher created a website showing a photo of Nick D'Augustine's face superimposed on a pornographic image and another manipulated to show a penis attached to D'Augustine's head.

Boucher confessed that his actions may have been wrong but said that he was trying to even the score with D'Augustine, whom he accused of trying to ruin his business.

Boucher said, 'My mistake was I stooped to his level.'

# The Last Laugh

## Mobile Madness

A young man bought his blonde wife a cell phone for their first wedding anniversary.

She was thrilled.

The next day at the mall, her phone rang. 'Hi Honey. How do you like your new phone?' he asked.

'I love it,' she replied, 'But there's just one thing I don't understand.'

'What's that, Baby?'

'How in the heck did you know I was at Wal-Mart?'

## Business Hot Shot

A young businessman had just started his own firm. He rented a beautiful office and had it furnished with antiques.

Sitting there, he saw a man come into the outer office. Wishing to appear the hot shot, the businessman picked up the phone and started to pretend he had a big deal working.

He threw huge figures around and made giant commitments. Finally he hung up and asked the visitor, 'Can I help you?'

The man said, 'Yeah, I've come to activate your phone lines.'

## Progress

I recently saw a distraught young lady weeping beside her car.

'Do you need some help?' I asked.

She replied, 'I knew I should have replaced the battery in this remote door unlocker. Now I can't get into my car. Do you think they (pointing to a distant convenience store) would have a battery for this?'

'Hmmm, I dunno. Do you have an alarm, too?' I asked.

'No, just this remote thingy,' which she handed to me with the car keys.

As I took the key and manually unlocked the door, I replied, 'Why don't you drive over there and check about the batteries ... it's a long walk.'

## Computer Literacy

Customer: 'How fast will my COM ports go?'

Tech Support: 'How hard can you throw your computer?'

# Chapter Eight

# Revenge of and on the Powerful

*'Just vengeance does not call for punishment.'*
Pierre Corneille,
*French dramatist (1606–84)*

Much to the irritation of the rest of us, it seems that many of the fabulously rich and ubiquitously famous truly believe that they are above the law. Or simply that natural justice does not apply to them. Yet, it is just this sort of arrogant pride that comes before a monumental and often humiliating fall ... and as the old adage tells us, 'the bigger you are, the harder you fall.'

The editor of the *Guardian* newspaper, Alan Rusbridger, is reported to have said in 1999 when politician Jonathan Aitken was sent to prison for perjury, four years after lying during his libel case against the *Guardian*, who accused him of political corruption: 'Libel is not a game: it is too often used by the rich, the powerful and the crooked to suppress proper reporting and fair comment. No one using the law against others can complain if the law is, in turn, used against them.'

The following are a collection of David versus Goliath-style revenge stories where the David in point is striking a blow for 'the little man' everywhere – and the Goliath is the faceless, nameless image of the world's famous, rich and powerful people.

# David versus Goliath

Sometimes those who seem most unassailable can be humbled by the smallest gestures even from those that they consider the lowest of the low.

## Miserable Failure

In a stand for the little man or to make a political statement (or for a bit of fun, one suspects), some people are getting one over on not one but two influential and powerful institutions – internet search engine companies and the president of the United States.

In December 2003, unknown persons manipulated search engine results so that the top-ranked page in Google when users searched on the phrase 'miserable failure' was the biography of President George W Bush from the White

House website. Remarkable, since the phrase 'miserable failure' doesn't even appear in the president's biography.

Apparently, this came about when a personal blog site urged others to include links connecting the phrase 'miserable failure' with the president's biography in their own websites and blogs. This is known as 'Google bombing', but since no user was hurt by the deed Google saw no need to take action.

## Dry Cleaning Bill

From: Amner, Jenny

Sent: 03 June 2005 10:25

To: Phillips, Richard

cc: *LON – ALL USERS 3RD FLOOR

Subject: RE: Ketchup trousers

With reference to the email below, I must apologise for not getting back to you straight away but due to my mother's sudden illness, death and funeral I have had more pressing issues than your £4.

I apologise again for accidentally getting a few splashes of ketchup on your trousers. Obviously your financial need as a senior associate is greater than mine as a mere secretary. Having already spoken to and shown your email and Anne-Marie's note to various partners, lawyers and trainees in ECC&T and IP/IT, they kindly offered to do a collection to raise the £4. I however declined their kind offer but should you feel the urgent need for the £4, it will be on my desk this afternoon.

Jenny

-----Original Message-----
From: Phillips, Richard
Sent: 25 May 2005 15:27
To: Amner, Jenny
Subject: Ketchup trousers

Hi Jenny

I went to a dry cleaners at lunch and they said it would cost £4 to remove the ketchup stains. If you cd let me have the cash today, that wd be much appreciated.

Thanks
Richard

Richard Phillips
Senior Associate
Commercial Department
Baker & McKenzie
100 New Bridge Street
London EC4V 6JA

*The above email correspondence between secretary, Jenny Amner, and senior associate, Richard Phillips, of the international law firm Baker & McKenzie speaks volumes. The story, which can be found on the internet, is said to be true, although the history of what took place originally is not made clear and we have no way of knowing whether or not these characters really exist. True or apocryphal, this senior associate is made to look small in the politest but most powerful of ways.*

## Queen of Mean

Leona Helmsley, the US businesswoman dubbed 'the Queen of Mean', was quoted in the newspapers as saying, 'We don't pay taxes. Only the little people pay taxes.'

She was sentenced in 1992 to four years in prison and fined $7.1 million for tax evasion.

## Church Shenanigans

A pupil was attending an end-of-term church service at his school accompanied by his father and his new, much-hated stepmother. Showing her disdain for the whole procedure, the stepmother proceeded to read her crime novel throughout the service.

The boy was so furious that he grabbed the book and ripped the last two pages out – destroying them in the process – so at least she never knew the ending.

## Thanks for Calling

A guy 'got revenge' on his credit card company when they gave him a charge of £25. The company sent him a letter notifying him of the charge, and giving him a free 0800 number to call in the event of any queries. He called the number and spent ten minutes on hold, which was when he realised that he was costing the company for the call. So he then attached a hands-free headset, and spent three entire days at work calling the 0800 number and hanging up once he got through, adding up to some 20 hours on hold! As his hands were still free, he reasoned that it didn't take away from his job at all. By then he was sure he'd cost them at least the £25 in call charges. At the end of day three he finally spoke to them, and instead of asking about his own charge, asked for a loan quote in the post and hung up. He says their on-hold music was actually OK, and was a great substitute for the radio!

## Suitable Escorts

There are several versions of this urban myth circulating on the internet, one of which accredits the story to President Johnson. Although the details of the story change, the theme of a prejudiced and uppity person of power getting their just desserts is the same.

The colonel's wife had a reputation for calling on military agencies and demanding special services. The following conversation took place when she called the Marine Basic School in Quantico, VA:

'Good morning, the Basic School, how may I help you?'

'This is Colonel Whiting's wife. We're hosting a formal get-together at our home tomorrow night, and I need two lieutenants, tall and good-looking, to serve as escorts for my daughters, and they need to be here at six, you got that?'

'Yes, Sir. Two lieutenants, tall and good-looking, six o'clock, ma'am.'

Colonel's wife: 'And no damn Mexicans!'

'Right, ma'am. No damn Mexicans.'

The next night, at six o'clock, Mrs Whiting answered the knock at the door, and sure enough, there were two tall, good-looking Marine lieutenants standing there.

'We're here to escort your daughters, ma'am.'

'But you're both black. There must be some mistake.'

'No, ma'am,' one of the lieutenants spoke up, 'Captain Rodriguez never makes mistakes.'

## Identity Crisis

An award should go to the Virgin Airlines gate attendant in Sydney some months ago for being customer-focused, while making her point, when confronted with a passenger who probably deserved to fly as cargo.

A crowded Virgin flight was cancelled after Virgin's 767s had been withdrawn from service. A single attendant was rebooking a long line of inconvenienced travellers. Suddenly an angry passenger pushed his way to the desk. He slapped his ticket down on the counter and said, 'I *have* to be on this flight and it *has* to be *now*.' The attendant replied, 'I'm sorry, Sir. I'll be happy to try to help you, but I've got to help these people first, and I'm sure we'll be able to work something out.' The passenger was unimpressed. He asked loudly, so that the passengers behind him could hear, '*Do you have any idea who I am?*' Without hesitating, the attendant smiled and grabbed her public address microphone: 'May I have your attention please,' she began – her voice heard clearly throughout the terminal. 'We have a passenger here at Gate 14 *who does not know who he is*. If anyone can help him find his identity, please come to Gate 14.'

With the folks behind him in line laughing hysterically, the man glared at the Virgin attendant, gritted his teeth and said, 'F**k you!' Without flinching, she smiled and said, 'I'm sorry, Sir, but you'll have to get in line for that too!!'

## The Church

Men of the cloth are expected to wield their power wisely, but occasionally errors in judgement are made and when that happens, they are open to ridicule, disgrace and acts of revenge like everyone else.

## Altar Ego

The Romanian daily newspaper, 7 *Plus*, reported that Father Petrica Florea from Costesti convinced a local 17-year-old girl to seduce a 74-year-old local councillor, Constantin Moise, on the altar of a local church while the priest filmed him in a plan to discredit the councillor.

The priest showed the film to his parishioners in the hope that the councillor would lose his job as a result, and the priest could step into his shoes. However, the plan backfired – his flock were so shocked that they chased the priest from the church and called the police.

## Deepest, Darkest Africa

In May 2006, while on an official tour of Kenya, the bishop of Chelmsford, the Right Revd John Gladwin, and 20 curates were abandoned in a wild and remote area of the central highlands. The archbishop of Kenya, the Most Reverend Benjamin Nzimbi, withdrew his hospitality with no notice when he learned of Bishop Gladwin's support for homosexuals in the Church.

Ultimately, their differences were patched up and the bishop's party resumed its tour, but not before a worrying day and night were spent in the wilderness.

## Missionary Disagrees with Cannibals

In this story, the boot is on the other foot and it is the family of a clergyman who have the vengeful satisfaction of the last laugh after their forebear suffered at the hands of others who had power over him.

In 2003, contrite villagers from Navatusila, Fiji were apologising to the descendants of Revd Thomas Baker in the hope that it would break a curse which they believed was on them due to the actions of their cannibal ancestors.

In 1867, the 35-year-old missionary of the Wesleyan Methodist Church was cooked and eaten by the villagers' forebears and the only things left of him were his leather boots. The current villagers blamed these actions for their current impoverished existence and they were hoping that if Revd Baker's descendants came to a special ceremony of atonement, things might change for the better.

# The Law

More than anyone else, those who work within the law have to uphold its values – or pay the price.

## Impartial Judgement

A judge in Germany is in big trouble after he fell for a defendant's girlfriend and sent her a text offering to 'lock him up for a long time'.

The girlfriend showed the messages to her boyfriend's lawyer. The judge was taken off the case and was facing disciplinary action and a possible charge of abuse of office, which carries up to five years in prison.

## Working up an Appetite

A farmer in Cumbria was rumoured to indulge in a physical relationship with his favourite cow when drunk.

After one particularly heavy drinking session, he was caught 'red handed' with the cow and the police were called. The farmer was thrown in the cells overnight to sleep it off.

Next morning, the farmer had sobered up and he was banging on his cell door demanding breakfast – apparently starving after his night's activities.

Finally, the door opened and a policeman shoved a plate of grass towards him, saying, 'If it's good enough for your girlfriend, it should be good enough for you.'

## Dog Food

The strangest tale of revenge and double revenge comes from Barnaul in Siberia where a policeman has been sentenced to five years in prison for killing a man.

Straightforward you might think ... but the sentence was on the lenient side because the court apparently took into account the fact that the policeman's victim had killed and then eaten his neighbour's dog.

When the police were called to the scene of the crime, they found the neighbour and his friends completely drunk – and they wouldn't open the door. The policeman broke in using an axe and, when the drunken pooch-muncher would not wake up, he kicked him several times – giving the man fatal internal injuries.

The policeman was found guilty of intentionally inflicting grievous bodily harm resulting in death and of abuse of power.

# Politicians

I don't expect you'll be giving this lot much sympathy – funny how everyone thinks that politicians have it coming!

## Turncoat Parrot

An Indian politician who had a parrot trained to sing his praises has been double-crossed.

The politician's arch rival Nitish Kumar enjoyed sweet revenge when, after years of hearing the parrot chanting 'Long Live Laloo' at meetings in support of Laloo Prasad Yadav of the National People's Party, the parrot started chanting 'Long Live Nitish' – without any provocation, according to his handler. Purely coincidentally, the trainer had recently changed his allegiances from Mr Yadav's party to that of his political opponent, Mr Kumar.

## Kiss 'n' Tell

When Edwina Currie published her *Diaries 1987–92*, she spilled the beans on an affair 14 years previously with the then prime minister, John Major. Some wondered why she had taken so long to go public with the affair but book reviewer Geordie Grieg for the *Observer* suggests, 'Her endgame … is twofold: revenge and vanity. She was furious to have missed out on Major's ascent, to have been brushed aside for promotion, and then the final humiliation: to have been airbrushed out of his memoirs.'

*Paradoxically, the British public who always considered Major as the Grey Man, seem to have warmed to the former PM since the disclosure that he was a philanderer – or was it the blue underpants that thawed our hearts?*

## Rising Above It

American Pulitzer-winning newspaper man, Ralph McGill said of Eleanor Roosevelt's critics and detractors: 'One of the shameful chapters of this country was how so many of the comfortable – especially those who profited from the misery of others – abused her ... But she got even in a way that was almost cruel. She forgave them.'

## Catty Quote of the Day

**Broadcaster and writer Sir Clement Freud described Margaret Thatcher as: 'Attila the Hen.'**

## Payback Time

In the US, it's not uncommon for legislators to propose a 'payback' bill in revenge for a proposed piece of legislation that annoys them.

In the late 1970s, delegate Frederick C Rummage from Prince George's County, Maryland, introduced a bill that would have created a commission to study the feasibility of gambling. It would also have converted Ocean City into 'a centre for legalised gambling'.

Russell O Hickman, the appalled delegate representing that intended coastal gambling destination, responded by introducing a bill that would have created a commission to study the feasibility of legalising prostitution – and convert Rummage's county into 'a centre for legalised prostitution'.

*Touché.*

## See You and Raise You

When George Bernard Shaw sent former prime minister Sir Winston Churchill a caustic invitation, reading: 'Am reserving two tickets for you for my premiere. Come and bring a friend – if you have one', Churchill replied, 'Impossible to be present for the first performance. Will attend second – if there is one.'

## Political Banishment

After Russian oligarch Mikhail Khodorkovsky declared his opposition to President Vladimir Putin he was arrested for fraud and tax evasion and sentenced to eight years in prison in a remote Siberian prison colony for fraud and tax evasion.

Far from silencing the former oil tycoon, his incarceration has made Khodorkovsky determined to launch a career in politics when he is released.

*Perhaps an oil tycoon would have been an easier opponent than an evangelical politician bent on political reform – and revenge?*

## Meltdown of The Iron Lady

According to a range of political memoirs, in 1989 Prime Minister Margaret Thatcher took her revenge on Chancellor

Nigel Lawson and Foreign Secretary Geoffrey Howe for forcing her to agree the circumstances in which she would join the European Monetary Union. She demoted Howe and undermined Lawson, forcing his resignation.

A year later, Sir Geoffrey Howe gave a devastating resignation speech in the Commons in which he attacked Thatcher – which opened the door for Michael Heseltine to announce his leadership challenge.

Howe's revenge effectively sounded the death knell of Thatcher's political reign.

## Miscalculation

A German politician misjudged a spontaneous publicity stunt when he poured champagne over the head of a homeless man as he opened a wine festival in Bremen. He reportedly laughed as he said, 'Here, now you have something to drink too!'

However, the crowd started booing the politician and his bodyguards tried to bundle the drenched man away. To make amends, the tactless politician then made matters worse by offering his victim some money and his expensive Mont Blanc pen, and even to put him up for a night in a hotel. However, the man declined his offers. Later that night, the politician resigned and offered a public apology.

# Celebs and Other People in the Public Eye

In an era where the public are obsessed with the minu-
tiae of a celebrity's life, it is hard for the rich and famous
to do anything without it being reported in magazines
and newspapers ... so if they decide to dabble in a
spot of revenge, we should be the first to hear about it,
wouldn't you think?

## Hollywood Hellcat

When 1940s Hollywood siren Ava Gardner found out that
her then boyfriend Howard Hughes was spying on her, she
took his two front teeth out with a bronze ornament.

✂ ✂ ✂ ✂ ✂ ✂ ✂ ✂ ✂

## Catty Quote of the Day 2

**Ava Gardner famously said of ex-husband Frank Sinat-
ra's marriage to Mia Farrow, 'Hah! I always knew Frank
would end up in bed with a boy!'**

✂ ✂ ✂ ✂ ✂ ✂ ✂ ✂ ✂

## Turning the Tables

After the birth of their baby, Shiloh, Angelina Jolie and Brad Pitt found a very fitting revenge for the months and years of hounding by America's celebrity press. They decided to sell pictures of the new arrival to the highest bidder and all proceeds would go to charity.

On Saturday, 3 June 2006, magazine editors were summoned to the offices of a photo agency on a hot and humid New York evening and corralled into separate little offices, all of which lacked air-conditioning. It was nearly midnight before they were shown the pictures, and they were informed that they had just six hours (until 6 am) to place their bids. Naturally, no one slept.

Eventually, the winner was *People* magazine, who shelled out $4.1 million for the privilege of exclusive access to the first pictures of baby Jolie/Pitt.

*For me, this is the perfect revenge. How satisfying must it have been for the celebrity couple to raise that much money for charity in one night – and turn the tables by making the lives of their photo-hungry pursuers uncomfortable for once.*

## Typecast for Life

During the silent movie era, everyone wanted to work with the great Valentino, so imagine everyone's surprise when an unknown actress was chosen to play opposite Valentino in the film of the book *Blood and Sand*.

Don Pendleton, the author of the book, insisted on unknown Nita Naldi being cast in the role of Doña Sol, the female sadistic demon of the film, after his false teeth fell into her cleavage during an argument at a dinner party.

Nita Naldi says, 'Many others were up for this role, but I got it. He wouldn't have anybody else. I kept saying to him, "How dare you insult me? This woman is a monster; she's a sex maniac; she's a sadist, she's a horror, the worst type." And he kept answering that this would be his revenge. And it was. I never outlived it.'

## All Creatures Great and Small

After her painful divorce from husband of ten years Tom Cruise, Nicole Kidman behaved with admirable dignity and self-restraint. The actress did allow herself one small dig though, when she reportedly said that, after the split, she could at least wear high heels again. Cruise is a diminutive five foot seven while Kidman is a statuesque five foot ten.

## A Dish Best Served Cold

In 1998, the food critic Michael Winner was allegedly rude to the staff in one of celebrity chef Jean-Christophe Novelli's restaurants. The chef was not present at the time but he did not forget this behaviour.

Eight years later, when Mr Winner and his girlfriend made a reservation at the new Novelli gastropub, The White Horse in Harpenden, Hertfordshire, the French chef delighted in instructing his staff to tell Winner that he was not welcome.

## Blunt Words

After being labelled a publicity seeker for talking about getting together with singer James Blunt, Tara Palmer-Tomkinson hit back. She not only said that she was completely in the dark about the fact that he had a live-in girlfriend (Camilla Boler) but was furious that he had deceived her on the subject. She is quoted as saying, 'One thing I will say is I was never, ever, ever, ever, ever, ever told by James Blunt that there was a girlfriend.

'I am certainly not the type of person who would tread on somebody else's toes. I completely disrespect women who do that to other women.

'…One things for sure – he may have a reputation as a bit of a Casanova but he's not.'

*So put that in your pipe, James, and smoke it.*

## Film Star Revenge

In India's 2004 general election in the southern state of Tamil Nadu, an aggrieved film star sought revenge on a prominent politician who criticised his work.

Actor Rajnikanth asked his fans to take on Dr SS Ramadoss's PMK party because the politician had trashed the star's last film.

**Revenge of and on the Powerful**

If a film star in the West asked fans to boycott a political party, it probably would not cause much of a stir, but in movie-crazy Tamil Nadu actors have huge fan bases and this was a closely fought election, so politicians were taking the threat seriously.

However, the Tamil cinema superstar met his first Waterloo in politics – the PMK still triumphed with ease in all six contested seats.

## Tea with a Dash

Even celebrities can resort to getting even with ex-boyfriends but these confessions were made while the cameras were rolling.

During an airing of *Celebrity Big Brother* two contestants confessed to getting revenge on former boyfriends.

Faria Alam, ex-lover of Sven Goran Eriksson and FA chief Mark Palios, revealed that she once peed in an exboyfriend's cup of tea. She then explained that she watched her boyfriend drink the 'spiked' tea, saying, 'That was the best part.'

Jodie Marsh also told of how she once got her own back on a cheating boyfriend. She said: 'I had wicked revenge. I packed up all his laundry and put it outside my house with his dirty pants on top.'

## Sticky End

There was a Hollywood urban legend circulating in the early 1990s claiming that actress Sean Young used superglue on an intimate part of her then-boyfriend James Woods' anatomy to glue it to another part of his body during an exceptionally tempestuous break-up. Ms Young, who believes the story was started to get revenge on her by Woods himself, dismissed it as a lie in a 1993 *Playboy* interview.

## Game, Set and Match

'If I were married to you, I'd put poison in your coffee,' Lady Astor notoriously said to Winston Churchill.

He, quick as a flash, replied, 'If you were my wife, I'd drink it.'

## Christmas Spirit

In his autobiography, former footballer Paul Gascoigne tells of a running battle of pranks with his old friend, nicknamed Five Bellies. After one particular incident, Gazza decides to get his own back with a really dirty trick.

He carefully took the lid off a mince pie (obviously a popular prop in the arsenal of weapons available to revenge-seekers), removed the filling and replaced it with dog s★★t. He then replaced the pie in the box and left it for Five Bellies to discover in the worst possible way.

## Taking it Hard

When Brenna Cepelak's affair with golf supremo Nick Faldo ended, presumably unhappily, she smashed up his Porsche with a golf club.

# Marilyn Monroe

There are numerous conspiracy theories surrounding the untimely death of Marilyn Monroe from an overdose of the drug Nembutal.

One of the theories most commonly cited is that proposed by Chuck Giancana, brother of the famous Chicago mob boss, Sam Giancana, in his 1992 book, *Double Cross*. He says that the Mafia killed Marilyn in order to gain revenge against the Kennedys, who had not rewarded the mob after JFK came to power despite their previous connections and the help the Mob may have given the Kennedys during the election campaign.

The theory goes that Giancana had Marilyn killed in order to implicate and embarrass Bobby Kennedy, but a neat little cover-up ensued.

## Music Industry Discord

In modern hip-hop, rappers notoriously engage each other in a very public war of words. These verbal feuds, often referred to as 'Beef', can get very nasty with some occasionally escalating into violence and even murder.

The most high-profile feud in rap was between Tupac Shakur and Notorious Big and their supporters. There were attacks and shootings followed by revenge attacks on and by the friends of each icon. Finally, the Tupac-Notorious Big feud culminated with the highly publicised assassinations of Tupac Shakur in 1996 and the revenge murder of Notorious Big the following year.

Although this brought the long-running feud to its obvious conclusion, there are still other notable hip-hop feuds rumbling on, including 50 Cent and Ja Rule; Eminem and Benzino; and Jay Z and Nas.

✂ ✂ ✂ ✂ ✂ ✂ ✂ ✂ ✂

# Boot on the Other Foot

Although it's true that the behaviour of celebrities and public figures is open to our scrutiny, there are those who live their lives in the public eye who are not able to openly answer their critics or accusations. But where there's a will, there's a way.

## We Are Not Pleased

Until 1996, the BBC had sole responsibility for producing the Queen of England's annual Christmas Day message. However, in 1997, the BBC aired an interview with Diana, Princess of Wales in which she talked candidly to Martin Bashir about her failed marriage to Prince Charles. It was watched by 21 million viewers.

Shortly after the interview was broadcast, Buckingham Palace announced that rival channel ITV would be producing the 1997 and 1998 Christmas messages. The explanation from the palace was that it was keen to bring ITV on board to try out fresh ideas.

However, internal BBC memos from the time clearly show that BBC executives believed the decision was a way to penalise the corporation for airing the Bashir interview.

Naturally, the Queen made no comment.

# The Last Laugh

## Abuse of Power

'If there are any idiots in the room, will they please stand up' said the sarcastic lecturer.

After a long silence, one freshman rose to his feet. 'Now then mister, why do you consider yourself an idiot?' enquired the lecturer with a sneer.

'Well, actually I don't,' said the student, 'but I hate to see you standing up there all by yourself.'

## Wait Your Turn

George Phillips of Meridian, Mississippi was going up to bed when his wife told him that he'd left the light on in the garden shed, which she could see from the bedroom window.

George opened the back door to go to turn off the light but saw that there were people in the shed stealing things.

He phoned the police, who asked, 'Is someone in your house?' and he said no. Then they said that all patrols were busy, and that he should simply lock his door and an officer would be along when available.

George said, 'Okay,' hung up, counted to 30, and phoned the police again.

'Hello I just called you a few seconds ago because there were people in my shed. Well, you don't have to worry about them now cause I've just shot them all.' Then he hung up.

Within five minutes three police cars, an Armed Response unit, and an ambulance showed up at the Phillips residence. Of course, the police caught the burglars red-handed. Then one of the policemen said to George: 'I thought you said that you'd shot them!'

George said, 'I thought you said there was nobody available!'

## Carnal Desires

A man is driving down a deserted stretch of highway when he notices a sign out of the corner of his eye. It reads: 'Sisters of St Francis House of Prostitution: 10 Miles'.

He thinks it was a figment of his imagination and drives on without a second thought. Soon he sees another sign, which says: 'Sisters of St Francis House of Prostitution: 5 Miles'.

Suddenly, he begins to realise that these signs are for real. Then he drives past a third sign saying: 'Sisters of St Francis House of Prostitution: Next Right'.

His curiosity gets the better of him and he pulls into the drive. On the far side of the car park is a stone building with a small sign next to the door reading 'Sisters of St Francis'.

He climbs the steps and rings the bell. The door is answered by a nun in a long black habit who asks, 'What may we do for you, my son?'

He answers, 'I saw your signs along the highway, and was interested in possibly doing business.'

'Very well, my son. Please follow me.'

He is led through many winding passages and is soon quite disoriented. The nun stops at a closed door and tells the man, 'Please knock on the door.'

He does as he is told and another nun in a long habit, holding a tin cup, answers the door. This nun instructs, 'Please place £100 in the cup, then go through the large wooden door at the end of this hallway.' He gets £100 out of his wallet and places it in the second nun's cup.

He trots eagerly down the hall and slips through the door, pulling it shut behind him. As the door locks behind him, he finds himself back in the parking lot, facing another small sign, which reads: 'Go in Peace. You have just been Screwed by the Sisters of St Francis. Serves you Right, you Sinner.'

# Chapter Nine
## Military Revenge

'No more tears now; I will think upon revenge.'
Mary Stuart,
Queen of Scots (1542–67)

It's probably fair to say that throughout history, wars, invasions and acts of territorial aggression have been motivated primarily by religion, greed or revenge. You only have to cast your mind back to your history classes to remember that in the 5th century BCE, Alexander the Great's conquest of Persia took place as a Greek revenge for the Persian ransacking of Greek towns. Another classic example is Caracalla's massacre of the citizens of Alexandria, which he ordered because they 'insulted' him. Not to mention Hannibal and his brothers who were brought up and indoctrinated by their father specifically to wreak revenge on Rome for the Carthaginian defeat in the First Punic War.

Sadly, 2,000 years on we're still repeating the same

vengeful cycle of international aggression followed by retaliation, despite notable world leaders and eminent figures eschewing such tactics. It was the American black leader and Nobel Prize winner Martin Luther King Jr who said, 'Mankind must evolve for all human conflict a method which rejects revenge, aggression and retaliation. The foundation of such a method is love.'

But rather than focus on military revenge on a grand scale, we're going to look here at how the armed forces offer the perfect arena for individual servicemen and women to wreak revenge on each other.

# With All Due Respect, Sir

Those unfamiliar with the forces might be forgiven for assuming that servicemen and women blindly follow orders and have no opportunity for dissent or disobedience. But anyone who has had any dealings at all with the military will tell you that the enlisted men and junior ranks are ingenious at finding ways to get back at superior officers – or inexperienced junior officers.

## Do as You Would Be Done By
The aircraft engine mechanics worked on the airstrip from early morning to late at night. Dressed in work

gear and kept at full working pace, the general understanding was that they would salute the officer in charge
as they began their shift, rather than every time an officer
happened to pass.

A new young pilot officer arrived one day, freshly famil-
iar with regulations. An LAC (leading aircraftsman) walked
past him and nodded acknowledgement. The pilot officer
called him back. 'Don't you know that you are supposed to
salute an officer when you pass him?'

'Yes, Sir' replied the LAC.

'Then you will salute me 100 times for failing to salute an
officer!' replied the fervent young officer.

The mechanic put down the engine parts he was carrying and duly saluted the pilot officer 100 times. Just as he
was about to pick up his load again, a voice called from a
distant senior officer who had observed the whole scene.
'For the record,' he said to the young pilot officer, 'you do
know that a salute is only valid when it is returned?'

The point was made and the pilot officer found himself
returning 100 salutes.

## Nagging Worry

A wife of the regimental colonel was always making life difficult for the junior officers. She was always nagging them
or on their case for something. At a formal dinner, the colonel's wife arrived at the function at the same time as some

of the junior officers. As they ascended to the dinner in the lift, she launched into one of her customary tirades. What she didn't realise was that as she was in full flow, so was one of the young officers – he was peeing in her handbag behind her back!

## Men in Tights

During National Service a young ballet dancer was conscripted into the RAF. At every chance the drill staff would ridicule him in front of his peers. For weeks he said nothing. One day, he challenged the drill sergeants to join him for his morning work-out before breakfast 'to see if the exercises were up to army standards'.

They readily agreed, expecting another opportunity to ridicule. The half hour of gruelling ballet exercises was more than a match for the sergeants, who emerged shattered and sobered by the experience, to the cheers of the entire billet.

## Running Out of Rope

A young officer had taken his men on an outdoor activity exercise. When it came to the abseiling exercise, 'Moose', as the officer was known, watched the men scaling down a rock face, until it was his turn.

While he was getting ready, he didn't notice that some of the men were shortening the rope by several feet. Moose lowered himself over the edge of the cliff. As he neared the ground, he suddenly ran out of rope and dropped the last six feet, landing in a heap on the floor.

The men claimed to know nothing about it, of course.

## Mail Pride

The men of 27G Flight were out on the drill yard when the mail arrived. It was raining hard and an hour of hard drill had already been completed. In a particularly vindictive mood, the corporal ordered the mail to be thrown on the wet ground, to be collected by the men when they had completed a fully correct drill routine.

Seeing their mail getting soaked and their short opportunity to read it being removed from them, the squad to a man took coordinated control. At every order, the men exercised a contrary move – left instead of right, forward instead of halt, etc. Within minutes, the whole scene was in disarray – every other squad and drill sergeant on the parade square stopped to witness the scene – orders being barked and responded to precisely but incorrectly by the angry squad.

Eventually the squad came to a halt in front of the saturated letters and remained at attention. Finally the order was given for 'at ease' then 'collect mail', and the dignified men obeyed quietly. Nothing more was said.

## Possession is Nine Tenths of the Law

During World War II, in the North African arena, a small group of British Special Forces soldiers arrived in an area newly acquired by the Allied Forces. They came across a US camp, neatly set up, but the men were out on manoeuvres.

Having been travelling light for months, and reasoning that the Yanks had it easy and deserved a lesson in military hardship, they helped themselves to a number of tents and melted back into the night.

## Inviting Disaster

The corporal was known for inventing extra menial tasks for the men. The order came for the men to make certain that the corporal was brought an early morning mug of tea. 'Do we wake you up, Sir?' was the question.

'If I'm not already awake,' came the self-assured answer, 'Then you can throw the tea over me!'

When it came to aircraftsman 'M's turn to take the tea, he had made good preparations. He walked with socks and no boots carefully to the corporal's room. He had oiled the door handle and hinges the day before. He turned the handle very slowly, opened the door noiselessly and, select-ing the boards which did not creak, carefully walked across to the bed where the corporal lay sound asleep. The rest is soggy history!

## Glencoe Massacre

The massacre of the MacDonald's of Glencoe is one of the most notorious examples of a scandalous blood feud in Scottish history.

In 1691 all Highland clan chiefs were required to swear and sign an oath of loyalty to the new protestant King William III by no later than 1 January 1692.

The penalties against those who failed to do so would be ferocious, and carried out with the full backing of the law. These would include the forfeiture of all lands, the destruction of their homes, the outlawing of their entire families and even murder at will.

Wisely, most clan chiefs decided it was prudent to sign the oath by the appointed time. However, Maclain of Glencoe, the elderly head of a small branch of the MacDonalds, failed to show by the deadline. Unfortunately, the poor chap had gone to the wrong place and so arrived at the appointed site a day late.

This was all the excuse that those in power needed to teach the highlanders a lesson. Secretary of State for Scotland John Dalrymple of Stair came up with a murderous plan, sanctioned by the king himself. However, for the plan to work, it relied on the duplicity of the MacDonalds' sworn enemies in a long-running blood feud, the Campbells.

On 1 February 1692 the Earl of Argyll's troops arrived in Glencoe under the command of Captain Robert Campbell. Despite the long-running vendetta between the two families, the MacDonalds were bound by tradition to refuse no visitor hospitality. So, however begrudgingly, the Campbell troops were invited into MacDonald homes where they were given food, drink and somewhere to stay.

For four days the Campbells enjoyed full MacDonald hospitality while awaiting their orders to arrive. Finally, the command came to butcher every man, woman and child under the age of 70. There was to be no mercy for any amongst this 'sept of thieves'.

On the evening of 5 February, Captain Robert Campbell dined with Maclain and his wife. Next morning, his men fell upon the unsuspecting MacDonalds and slaughtered 38 of them. Countless others were forced into the snow-topped Scottish mountains where many died.

The attack was condemned in the Scottish parliament and led to the fall of the government of the Earl of Stair. However, the longer-lasting effect was that the actions of the Campbells fuelled the feud between them and the MacDonalds to the extent that there is still friction to this day.

# Experience Pays

Young British army officers join their battalions fresh from Sandhurst Military College full of enthusiasm and theory – and these wet-behind-the-ears young men immediately outrank soldiers who have years of experience in the ranks. However, the seasoned soldiers always find ways to get even with those inexperienced officers who try to make life difficult for them.

## Borrow Mine, Sir

An uppity or over-eager officer will be the target on exercise of an old trick. One of the men will surreptitiously swipe the officer's binoculars. Someone else who is in on the trick will point out something 'of interest' in the distance. When the young officer cannot lay his hands on his binoculars, a helpful soldier will offer to lend him his own pair. Unbeknownst to the officer, the eye-sockets of the binoculars have been smeared in boot polish, so the unsuspecting young man ends up looking like a panda.

## Nasty Break

When on field exercises a latrine and a cesspit are dug. It is army practice to place a spade on the edge of the cesspit to which you hold on while hanging your backside over the pit in order to evacuate your bowels.

The men have been known to partially saw through the handle of the spade before a disliked young officer goes to the loo – with obviously very smelly results.

## Ringing in the Ears

Guardsmen get even with the young officers or unpopular fellow soldiers in the Cavalry regiments by hiding an alarm clock inside their Busby, timed to go off at the most embarrassing time – usually on parade.

## The Officer Knows Best

A new RAF officer in charge of the aircraft servicing crew was not given to listening to the experience of the ground crew. Despite other urgent jobs, a senior aircraftsman was detailed to clean 500 pairs of centrifugal oil cleaners for the aircraft engines.

It took four days of intensive work, as the aircraftsman worked to the specific instructions of the officer.

After four days, he took the service sheet to the officer for his signature. Job complete according to instructions and signature in place, the aircraftsman then pointed out the small print in the servicing manual which the officer had failed to notice when giving his precise instructions.

Each oil cleaner had to be pressure cleaned in a special chamber before being reassembled! The job had to be

completely redone. Four valuable days had been wasted
– and the officer was accountable.

## Lost Something?

While on exercise, the men watch carefully for a disliked officer to go off into the bushes for a Number Two.
They quietly follow him, and when he squats down to
perform they carefully place a long-handled spade under
his backside.

When he's finished, the men pull the spade away. The
officer stands up and turns to cover up his message with soil
but there is nothing there.

It causes much confusion and embarrassment for the
young officer – and much mirth for the men.

## Samurai Code

This aristocratic warrior class from Japan's feudal past were
duty-bound to uphold the honour of their family, clan or
their lord by *katakiuchi*, which roughly translated means
revenge killings.

This practice flourished in Japan right up to the opening of the country to the West. Those who killed another
person were not subject to punishment if they could show
that their actions were justified as *katakiuchi*.

Although officially outlawed in 1873, the practice of
*katakiuchi* did not stop then. Some historians say that an

incident in 1880 probably marked Japan's last blood revenge. A father, Fukuoka, was killed when his son Rokuro Usui was only six years old. However, when he was 22, Rokuro exacted revenge by tracking down his father's killer – a once radical samurai who had become a successful senior government official – and assassinated him. Rokuro was sentenced to life in prison.

# Police

Nobody relishes the thought of finding themselves in the clutches of the long arm of the law but, judging from the following stories, it's not always a barrel of laughs if you cross another policeman – even if you're in the force yourself.

## Cat Burglar?

PC 'T' couldn't stand cats. He and another PC were walking along the deserted high street on a quiet night shift when he was startled by a cat jumping off a wall on to his shoulder. In sheer terror and fury, PC 'T' hurled his truncheon at the cat, 'That'll teach you …' But the truncheon bounced off the road and straight through the plate glass window of a department store!

This was in the olden days before alarms or mobile phones. How to explain the presence of his truncheon inside a shop window? It was too far inside to reach by hand. Initiative was called for – and a couple of props.

They knew they would find clothes props in the nearby back lane, so the policemen duly borrowed two in the line of duty. They retrieved the truncheon with the giant chopsticks through the broken glass, returned the implements to their rightful owners and rang in to report a break-in at the shop.

The owners were immensely grateful that the police had been at the right place at the right time and scared the burglars away!

## I'm Spartacus

It was mandatory to sign the book for every action taken. Failure to do so could result in loss of a day's pay. The superintendent called the shift to task. 'There is a space without a signature in yesterday's entries! I want to know who is responsible.'

Silence.

'I expect to see a signature in that place before the end of the shift!'

At the end of the shift he went to inspect the book. In the two-inch slot that had been empty he found 11 signatures – every man on the shift had signed.

## Watching and Waiting

In the days before mobile phones, the police had a series of locked phone boxes. Any shift 'beats' would include regular 'rings' to the police station switchboard, so that central control knew roughly where every beat policeman was. One inspector was a stickler about times of the rings. He would meet up randomly with the police on the beat, checking to see if they were where they should be and weren't sheltering in a police box having a smoke or a bite of lunch! His favourite trick was to watch the police boxes and time how long a PC was inside, reporting them if they were longer than the time needed to ring in. To be reported meant the loss of a day's pay.

PC 'M' was on the beat one cold snowy January day. Being an observant PC he noticed the inspector at a distance down the road, being 'inconspicuous'. He knew he was under observation. He turned down the next street towards the police box. The snow was freshly fallen and every footprint was clear. He made his call to the station, then stepped carefully backwards out of the police box into his own footprints, reversing down the pathway until his prints crossed some others. Then he waited up a back lane. As anticipated, the inspector turned into the street and saw the footprints leading to the box. He checked his watch and waited ... and waited ... and waited.

PC 'M' left him to wait and continued checking his

properties on the beat. Thirty minutes later, he returned to the street for another ring and found the inspector still waiting to catch him when he left the police box. 'Afternoon, Sir! Waiting for me, Sir? I rang in half an hour ago.' How the inspector explained his half hour wait outside an empty police box was never revealed to PC 'M', but the inspector never reported any PCs again.

# Pulling Rank

Sadly, some members of the armed forces are not above using their superior rank to get even with those who cross them.

## True Love Never Runs Smooth

During the World War II, Eileen, a 24-year-old London woman, was attached to the Royal Engineers & Mechanical Engineers (REME) Corps at Woolwich, assigned to repairing searchlights. A REME officer took a shine to the young woman and repeatedly asked her to go out with him. She declined, explaining that she had a boyfriend.

The officer discovered the boyfriend's name, and had him redeployed overseas.

## Career Block

Colonel 'X', a commanding officer of a battalion serving in Northern Ireland, was a bullying character who rode roughshod over his officers and men alike. There was one particular captain who refused to be intimidated by his heavy-handed tactics and who proved to be a constant thorn in the side of the bombastic colonel.

However, out of spite, when a perfect posting came along for the captain in question, the colonel refused to release him, arguing that the captain was essential to the running of his operation. He also blocked a secondment overseas for the young captain, who eventually resigned his commission.

✂ ✂ ✂ ✂ ✂ ✂ ✂ ✂ ✂

## Reparation

**There is an official military term for seeking revenge after a war that is called military reparation. This term refers to a situation where a country that has won a war seeks financial redress for the wrongs inflicted on it by the losing country. Thus the defeated state is obliged to pay damages to the victorious nation for the economic harm it inflicted during wartime.**

For example, under the military reparation terms of the Treaty of Versailles after the defeat of Germany in World War I, the Allies demanded that Germany deliver one eighth of its livestock and provide ships, trains and other materials to replace those it had destroyed during the war. Germany also had to provide France with large quantities of coal. In addition, the Allies expected Germany to pay annual sums of money to a total reparation of about $33 billion.

However, the big flaw in the principle of military reparation is that any defeated nation is almost certainly going to be in dire economic straits and probably unable to make any sort of redress. This was certainly the case with post-WWI Germany. Although the Allies and Germany renegotiated and reduced the reparation amounts, in reality, Germany could not and did not pay. Eventually, when Adolf Hitler came to power in Germany in 1933, he repudiated the Treaty of Versailles, and the rest, as they say, is history.

✂ ✂ ✂ ✂ ✂ ✂ ✂ ✂

# The Last Laugh

## T Shirt Saying

'I don't have a licence to kill. I have a learner's permit.'

## See You and Raise You

This internet joke is told as if it were the transcript of an actual radio conversation of a US naval ship with Canadian authorities off the coast of Newfoundland in October, 1995.

AMERICANS: Please divert your course 15 degrees to the North to avoid a collision.

CANADIANS: Recommend you divert YOUR course 15 degrees to the South to avoid a collision.

AMERICANS: This is the Captain of a US Navy ship. I say again, divert YOUR course.

CANADIANS: No. I say again, you divert YOUR course.

AMERICANS: This Is The Aircraft Carrier USS Lincoln, The Second Largest Ship In The United States' Atlantic Fleet. We Are Accompanied By Three Destroyers, Three Cruisers And Numerous Support Vessels. I Demand That You Change Your Course 15 Degrees North, That's One Five Degrees North, Or Counter-Measures WILL Be Undertaken To Ensure The Safety Of This Ship.

CANADIANS: This is a lighthouse. Your call.

AP Out.

## Due Respect

A defence contractor finally succeeded in building a computer capable of solving the most complex naval warfare problems. The top brass assembled around the new machine and were instructed to feed a difficult tactical problem into it. They described a complex hypothetical battle situation to the computer and then asked the pivotal question, 'Should our forces attack or retreat?'

The computer hummed and beeped for about an hour, and finally printed out an answer, 'Yes.'

The senior officers stared at each other, mystified by the response.

Finally, one of them submitted a second request to the computer, 'Yes what?'

The computer responded instantly, 'Yes, Sir!'

# Chapter Ten
# Student Revenge

'[Revenge] is sweeter far than flowing honey.'
The Iliad, *Homer (c. 900–850 BCE)*

The education system has always provided rich pastures for stories of revenge, ranging from the school kids who set off fire-alarms to disrupt exams or who play spiteful pranks on much disliked teachers to the educators who find pointless errands or plan detentions for those kids who have rubbed them up the wrong way.

Every teacher can probably recount a story of when a student has tried to get even. In the main, the revenge takes the harmless form of a pupil who bears a grudge playing a misguided joke or prank – in days gone by, balancing a bucket of water above a door in anticipation of the teacher's entrance was considered risqué.

But in recent years revenge has assumed a new dimension

# Student Revenge

with the appearance of the internet and with the arrival of online sites dedicated to students who want to have their say about teachers. This rather sinister development gives students an opportunity to publicly but anonymously sully a teacher's name and reputation, for whatever reason.

As John Reinan reports in the *Minneapolis Star Tribune*, American Dan Jancke, an art teacher, was suspended after accusations that he had sent sexually explicit emails to sixth-grade girls. After a police investigation, it soon became clear that two seventh-grade boys had posed as Jancke in an online chat with the girls.

Across the United States and Europe, teachers are suffering internet harassment daily and it simply adds to the stress of the profession. At Dulwich College in South London, students have created fake profiles for two teachers at the school, implying that one of the male teachers likes to dress as a woman. Most teachers I spoke to are philosophical about the problem, saying that sites such as ratemyteacher.com, where students can grade their teachers on a scale of one to five, together with critical comments and smiley or frowning faces, are simply an occupational hazard and that trying to block access to such sites is futile.

The stories that follow are more akin to the old-style, slapstick form of revenge in the mould of St Trinian's and Billy Bunter rather than the new technological approach.

# Students Seek Revenge on Other Students

Put a group of high-spirited young people together in the same institution, add hormones and petty rivalries, and what do you get? A boiling pot of pranks and tit-for-tat reprisals!

## Backfiring Revenge

Paul, a student studying architecture in New Zealand, came back to find his room completely trashed – clothes strewn everywhere, books littering the floor. He was distraught, particularly as he couldn't think of anyone who might want to do such a thing to him.

After a couple of weeks, the culprit came clean – it was a guy whom Paul didn't even know. The guy was seeking retribution on someone else and had mistakenly sacked the wrong room.

When a group of Paul's female friends found out about the blunder, they decided to exact their own revenge. They sent a picture of the room-trasher to the 'Wants To Meet' personal ads section of a gay magazine, giving his return postal address.

Up to two years later, the guy was still getting proposition letters, and he was not best pleased.

## Canned Laughter

Girls sharing a halls of residence at Cambridge University punish certain room-mates by piling tins of groceries outside their bedroom door so that when they come out bleary-eyed in the morning, they get the shock of their lives as the cans noisily scatter down the corridor.

## Liar, Liar, Pants on Fire

While at university, a vengeful girl let her unfaithful lover believe that she had given him a sexually transmitted infection by sprinkling a small dash of chilli powder plus some very tiny bits of chilli on his underwear.

He was conned and became increasingly paranoid as, when washed, the stain spread, leaving him to believe that the infection was spreading.

## Humble Apologies

A sorority house and a fraternity house were situated side by side on an American college campus. The frat held a party one night, and there was much drinking, rude behaviour and shouted obscenities, much of which was directed at the sorority house. The women were highly irritated, and to help smooth things over the next morning the fraternity sent over several boxes of doughnuts with their deepest apologies. The sorority members, still annoyed, accepted the peace offering and ate their free breakfast.

All was fine until one of the girls, at the next frat party, noticed the photos pinned to the bulletin board inside the frat house – the boys were wearing the doughnuts on the erect portions of their anatomy.

## Many Happy Returns

A second year student who had shared with the most annoying room-mate for over a year paid back the numerous insults and injuries he had suffered by surreptitiously borrowing his roomie's library card (left lying on the desk among books) and taking out an obscure book from the university library. He then disposed of the book and replaced the card on the desk.

The unfortunate student could not understand why he kept getting reminders and overdue notices for a book he had never even heard of. He maintained his innocence but was eventually forced to pay a hefty overdue fine and the cost of a replacement book.

## High Rise Horror

A group of students at Loughborough University decided to get their revenge on a fellow student who was much disliked for a variety of reasons. The guy lived in halls of residence on the 14th floor of the Tower. One night, a couple of students took the guy out and set about getting him drunk. Meanwhile, others in the revenge party set about removing everything from his room and reassembling it all in an empty room on the ground floor so that it looked identical.

They brought the transgressor home, blind drunk, and put him to bed in his new ground floor room. In the middle of the night, a group of them burst into his room, shouting, 'We've had enough of you. Let's throw him out of the window.'

The poor guy, who was still feeling pretty groggy, remonstrated with them, surely no one would throw him from the 14th floor. But they grabbed him and threw him through the window. He actually only fell five feet to the ground and was only bruised and scratched, but psychologically he was much more battered.

## Where Am I?

Student flatmates fall out – it happens. But one pair of teenage lads decided to get revenge on their female flatmate after a disagreement by bricking up her bedroom door while she was asleep inside the room.

## Shower Power

While taking a shower, a female student was locked in the bathroom after some male students put superglue in the bathroom lock.

The girls decided to pay the boys a revenge raid. They went to the boys' rooms and stole all of their clothes, which they then mixed up and hung on trees around the campus. Each male student was left solely with a thong, which the girls hung on a hanger in their bedrooms.

Adding to their problems, after recovering their clothing none of the boys could remember which items belonged to them!

# Students on Teachers

We're back to where we started with the following stories of the traditional underdog, the impotent student getting even with the power-wielding teacher. Hasn't it ever been thus?

## Spud Attack

In secondary schools across the land, it has been common practice for victimised pupils to get even with their tormentors by putting a potato up the exhaust pipe of the hated teacher's car. After starting the engine, the unsuspecting teacher will only get a few yards before the engine cuts out.

If you have partaken in this particular form of revenge, you're in good company: in the House of Commons Hansard Debates for 12 March 1999, Mr David Maclean (MP for Penrith and the Border) declares, 'I must confess – as a former law and order Minister, it is dangerous to make

such confessions – that, as a young child, on occasion I mis-
behaved by sticking a potato up an exhaust pipe to make a
vehicle grind to a halt.'

However, there is a story circulating that a teacher died
of carbon monoxide poisoning after a vengeful pupil played
this revenge trick on him because the exhaust pipe had a
hole in it and the car filled with exhaust fumes. You may
well have heard this story but, never fear, it is not true – just
another one of those urban myths.

## Teacher's Pet

When Julie Hunt, 43, from Maine, USA heard that a teacher
had given her daughter low marks, she agreed to help her
13-year-old get her own back by baking biscuits for the
teacher laced with laxatives.

However, the act of revenge backfired when the teacher
shared the biscuits among the daughter's classmates and four
of them fell ill, leading to Hunt's arrest.

## Disturbed Night

In 1962, John had put up with all sorts of rough treatment from
an over-zealous head boy. After he was given the strap on the
head boy's say-so, he decided it was time to get his own back.

So he rang the numerous taxi firms in the area and
organised for a taxi to turn up at the house of the head
boy's parents every hour through the night. No sooner had

they got to bed after one taxi driver had been sent away than another would turn up and ring the doorbell.

## Do You Know Who I Am?

A New Zealand television advertisement shows the apocryphal story of one young man's revenge on a pompous examiner.

The students were in an exam room. A young guy finished his paper and started doing a scratch card with his pen, just as the adjudicator said, 'One minute to go.'

When the examiner said, 'Time up. Put your pens down and bring your papers to the front desk,' the young man was still fiddling with his scratch card and only realised what was happening as the other students started filing out of the room. He gathered his things and rushed to the front desk with his paper.

The pompous and rather vindictive invigilator said in an off-hand manner, 'Sorry, you had plenty of warnings on time. You're too late. You've failed. Sorry.'

Keeping his cool, the young man said, 'Excuse me, do you know who I am?'

'I've no idea,' sneered the teacher condescendingly.

'Good,' replied the student and with that, he slipped his paper into the middle of the pile of completed papers and walked out, cheerily looking over his shoulder and enjoying his moment of sweet revenge.

## Dead Funny

When a school leaver left the Royal Grammar School in Newcastle upon Tyne for the last time, as his parting shot he arranged for some funeral directors to visit the home of his former much-loathed but very much alive headmaster.

## Invisible Writing

William, son of a horticulturalist and sixth form student at a well-known Scottish boarding school, used his father's specialist knowledge to get even with the headmaster he loathed.

Under the cover of darkness, William crept on to the front lawn of the headmaster's house (which was in the school grounds) and using sea salt, wrote certain expletives and insults across the turf.

Salt is one of the quickest ways to kill grass and the unfortunate headmaster had a few choice words clearly visible in brown, faded writing on his lawn for months to come.

## Lecherous Lecturer

In the 1990s, a New Zealand college lecturer had a reputation for being rather lecherous with the female students. Despite complaints about his inappropriate behaviour, his unwanted tactile attentions continued.

One day, the lecturer in question was found tied to a tree, stark naked and he had obviously been knocked about a bit.

The story of the female students' revenge made headline news.

## Post Script

In fact, so notorious was the case of the New Zealand lecturer's fate, that when something similar started happening some years later at another campus, it was enough for someone to place a placard in the grounds stating 'Remember' plus the name of the attacked lecturer as a warning.

## Easy Grades

In January 2006, history professor David Weale of Canada's University of Prince Edward Island offered B-minus grades to any students in his overcrowded class if they would just go away, and 20 of the 95 accepted.

However, some outraged students blew the whistle on Professor Weale and their co-students and when the administration found out, Professor Weale, who had retired the previous year but returned to teach that one course, was invited to re-retire.

## Bulls**t Baffles Brains

While at college, a star IT student was invited to develop and install a new mainframe payroll update system for an office. When the time came to introduce it, he couldn't resist telling the staff that the system had an advanced feature whereby it could read handprints off the screen to authenticate the user. So after they keyed in their usernames and passwords, they had to put their hands on the screen and hit enter. The cursor flashed across the screen, as if it was scanning the handprint, and then a message would welcome them to the system.

For about a week, all five office staff were putting their hands on the screen to log in. Then one day the student's boss happened to notice what they were doing; the colleagues were all very shamefaced they'd fallen for it!

## Careers Blocked

A group of masonry students in Denmark were so hacked off with the lack of internships available to them after qualifying that they built a wall across the entrance to the education ministry to make their point. Their plan was to let Bertel Haarder, the Danish education minister, see for himself how hard it is to enter the labour market.

## On the Move?

Having been given double-detention, unfairly as he felt, 15-year-old 'Peter' roped in a couple of his mates to help him get even with the harsh teacher who had dealt out the punishment.

Since he knew where she lived, he and his friends spent the night taking down all the 'For Sale' signs from houses in the local area and replanting them in her front garden. She woke up to a sea of signs from various estate agents littering her borders and lawn.

## St Trinian's

It's hard to believe now but in its day St Trinian's, a fictional girls' school populated by gin-swigging, well-armed pupils, was groundbreaking stuff. Until the cartoonist Ronald Searle's wayward characters appeared in the late 1940s and early 1950s, the stereotypical image of pupils at posh girls' boarding schools was of the peaches-and-cream, well-mannered young lady or the jolly-hockey-sticks, sporty, never-tell-a-fib head girl.

So the wicked and violent St Trinian's girls, who were hell-bent on dodgy deals and doling out retaliation to snitches and swots, and wreaking revenge on any teacher who gave them lines or interfered with their money-making schemes, was a shock to the British public.

Remarkably though, St Trinian's became hugely popular and was made into a series of comedy films starring Alastair Sim who played both the

# Student Revenge

headmistress (in drag) and her brother, George Cole as 'Flash Harry', and Joyce Grenfell as the harassed policewoman.

Siriol Hugh-Jones, a St Trinian's fan and reviewer, believes that women and girls, in particular, love the characters because, 'there were, and are, times when all they long for is a small bomb or a sharp little cleaver, and because the cartoons, for all the cheerful horror, are perhaps fundamentally on their side. Confiscate a girl's gin, ban her tobacco, she will still find a way to triumph over her environment ...'

For those of you who are unfamiliar with the cartoons or the films, here is an extract from a letter that the headmistress writes to an old college friend, describing the past term at St Trinian's. It gives a small insight into the anarchy that reigns and the vengeful mindset of the pupils:

... The American girl has made a great hit. I feared that her name (Gloria Milton Zimmermann) might be against her, but when she announced that she came from Chicago they were all over her. She has been most generous, nylons for the Sixth (and yours truly!), refrigerated steaks all round, and fearsome concoctions called Rye and Bourbon which have caused much merriment in the studies. She showed them how to wire a chair for electricity, and they put a sharp charge through Mademoiselle just as she was getting into her stride with a La Fontaine fable. The current was from the School plant, and obviously of no very damaging voltage, but Mademoiselle made the most ridiculous fuss ... Sometimes one really despairs of foreigners ...

November the Fifth was a merry affair, with bangs and explosions most of the day and a monster bonfire (of desks! but I didn't get ratty) as soon as dusk fell. One of the fireworks could not have been properly assembled and blew all the Vicarage windows out: it was just like dear old 1940. Our head girl, Rhoda Hornby (and a real fizzer), had a whip-round among the Juniors and soon netted the cash. She laughingly called it Entertainment Tax and everybody under fifteen had to stump up eighteen and sixpence. There was some grumbling but she scotched that pretty pronto! It was a fine example of leadership and initiative: Rhoda should make her mark at Girton.

# Teachers against Students

Stories of educators exacting revenge on troublesome students exist within the closed walls of staff rooms all over the world, but the teaching profession are not keen to let it be publicly known that they sink to the same levels as lesser mortals (known as students) in the pursuit of revenge – especially against kids. However, the odd revenge story leaks out – whether it was pre-meditated or otherwise.

## So Close

This particular student had troubled the dean of the college for the four years that she attended. On graduation day, the student walked on to the stage to collect her neatly scrolled, ribbon-bound diploma. Once she had the qualification in her hand, she leant across the podium and told the dean what she thought of her, in no uncertain terms – not only questioning her parenthood but also referring to her lack of physical allure.

When the student got home, feeling exceptionally pleased with herself, she unrolled her diploma to put in a frame on the wall. It read, 'In order to receive your diploma, please present this certificate to the dean of your college after final grades have been posted.'

# The Last Laugh

## I'll Eat My Words

The science teacher had to leave her classroom for a few minutes. On returning, she found the children in perfect order. Everybody was sitting absolutely quiet.

She was shocked and absolutely stunned. She said, 'I've never seen anything like it before. This is wonderful. But, please tell me, what came over all of you? Why are you so well behaved and quiet?'

Finally, after much urging, little Julie spoke up and said, 'Well, once you said that if you ever came back and found us quiet, you would drop dead.'

## Student's Revenge

Finding one of his Sunday school students making faces at others in church, Father Vesy stopped his sermon to reprove the child.

The priest said, 'Michael, when I was a child, I was told that if I made ugly faces, it would freeze and I would stay like that.'

Michael looked up and replied, 'Well, Father, you can't say you weren't warned.'

# Chapter Eleven
# The Worm Turns

'Surviving well is your finest revenge.'
Morgan Nito,
author (1869–1948)

When Professor Hans Crombag, emeritus professor of Psychology of Law, conducted research among psychology and law students at the University of Maastricht, it became clear that for those people who take revenge on others, the main reason was to make it clear that they would not be walked over. Still, although nearly two-thirds of respondents admitted that they had cause to take revenge in the past year, 71 per cent of them had not acted on the impulse.

According to the Maastricht study, most people consciously abandon thoughts of revenge, preferring to sort things out peacefully. Given that we all inherently know that most people won't retaliate, it comes as even more of a surprise when an unlikely person commits an act of cunning and unexpected revenge that leaves the victim reeling. Those who have put up with nonsense and abuse for years; those who have always been supportive and in the background; those who have never had a voice – these are the worms who finally turn and cause havoc.

Here we look at some unlikely suspects who turned out to be the ones responsible for some pretty sneaky acts of retribution.

# About Time Too

Isn't it strange how we tell our mild-mannered friends not to be a doormat or people will walk all over them … but when they finally snap and retaliate, we are always so shocked.

## Mud Slinging

After a series of what seemed to him nonsensical directives and initiatives, a farmer in the Morpeth area of Northumberland took matters into his own hands. He drove his tractor and silage trailer to the local council offices, and sprayed them with the contents.

## Sacred Characters

University of Pittsburgh student Brandon Smith wanted a tattoo that proclaimed his manliness, so he decided to get the Chinese characters for 'strength' and 'honour' on his chest. After 20 minutes under the needle of local tattoo artist Andy Sakai, he emerged with the symbol for 'small penis' embedded in his flesh.

'I had it for months before I knew what it really meant,' Smith said.

'Then I went jogging through the Carnegie Mellon campus and a group of Asian kids started laughing and calling me "Shorty". That's when I knew something was up.'

Sakai, an award-winning tattoo artist, was tired of seeing sacred Japanese words, symbols of his heritage, inked on random white people. So he used their blissful ignorance to make an everlasting statement. Any time a customer came to Sakai's home studio wanting Japanese tattooed on them, he modified it into a profane word or phrase.

'All these preppy sorority girls and suburban rich boys think they're so cool 'cause they have a tattoo with Japanese characters. But it doesn't mean shit to them!' Sakai said. 'The dumb-asses don't even realise that I've written "slut" or "pervert" on their skin!'

In 2003, at least seven people unknowingly received explicit tattoos from the disgruntled artist. Kerri Baker, a Carlow College freshman, paid $50 to have the symbols for 'beautiful goddess' etched above her belly button, but when she went into Szechuan Express Asian Noodle Shop sporting a bare midriff, the giggling employees explained to her that the tattoo really said, 'Insert General Tso's Chicken Here!'

'I don't even like General Tso's!' Baker sobbed. 'I'm a vegetarian!'

Sakai doesn't feel guilty about using hapless college students as canvases for his graffiti.

'I think I'm helping my fellow man by labelling all the stupid people in the world,' he explained. 'It's not a crime, it's a public service.'

## Post Script

You might think that Sakai learnt his lesson after being sentenced to five years in prison for inking profanities on hordes of hapless customers but you'd be wrong.

His latest act of revenge? Sakai has being doing tattoos for fellow inmates – and he's left dozens of hardened criminals with butterflies, fairies and unicorns permanently etched in their skin.

'I wanted a stack of skulls on my back,' said murderer Jimmy Drake, 'and that Asian prick gave me a giant Winnie the Pooh!'

For his own protection, Sakai has been moved to solitary confinement where he'll serve the rest of his sentence.

## Getting It Any Way She Can

When Guenther Kran lost his appetite for sex, his frustrated wife decided to look elsewhere, and took a job in a brothel. Adelheid, aged 58, of Berlin said, 'I like sex, I like it a lot, but my husband Guenther has no appetite for sex any more and does it about once a year.'

Rather than viewing her actions as revenge for ignoring her, Adelheid prefers to see her new job as a way of easing the tension between her and her husband, although she admits, 'Guenther is not thrilled about it, but I can't hem myself in just because he's not up for it.'

Ironically, she also reckons they are getting on better now than before she started working in the 'mature ladies' brothel.

## Doctor, Doctor

After repeated broken nights while on night duty, a doctor saw red when he was called out of bed on a fatuous night visit at 3 am – despite having assured the family that the call was not urgent or life-threatening.

The following night, whilst on a genuine early-morning call, he decided to visit the aforementioned time-waster to check they were 'all right.'

## Burn-out

A dutiful Saudi son was admitted to hospital for psychological treatment after his divorced parents forced him to marry four times within six months.

Firstly, the father insisted the boy should marry a girl from his side of the family. Then the mother retaliated by ordering him to wed a girl from her side, reports the *Al-Watan* daily newspaper.

Not content with that, the father insisted on a third wife from his side to restore the balance of power. So, you guessed it – the mother, not to be outdone, demanded that her son take another wife from her side of the family.

The son has sought refuge in hospital and is refusing to see his parents or his wives!

## In the Dog House

Zdislawa Bukarowicza was so fed up with her husband spending all their money on vodka and coming home drunk that she chained him up in the dog kennel and fed him on dog food and water for three weeks.

Despite temperatures of -20°C at his home in Scinawa, Poland, the 75-year-old survived and was eventually freed when his drinking-buddies, who hadn't seen him at their local for several days, called the police.

## Me Tarzan, You Aaaaagh

On a similar theme, another wife, this time in Romania, tired of her husband's drinking, locked him in the bedroom. But 66-year-old Stefan Trisca was not to be deterred by a locked door. Instead he tried to make his escape by swinging from tree to tree to get to the bar. But his plan backfired when he slipped from a vine and fell 15 feet to the ground, breaking his arm, an ankle and a leg.

'I didn't think it would be such a big deal to go from tree to tree and get down to the ground. Unfortunately, it was more difficult than it looked in the Tarzan movies,' confessed Mr Trisca.

Mrs Trisca declined to comment but she had a wry smile on her face.

## Mums Fight Back

A worm-turns story that is circulating by email.

An American woman, renewing her driver's licence at the Motor Vehicle's office, was asked by the clerk to state her occupation. She hesitated, uncertain how to classify herself. 'What I mean is,' explained the clerk, 'do you have a job or are you just a ...?'

'Of course I have a job,' snapped the woman. 'I'm a Mom.'

'We don't list "Mom" as an occupation, "housewife" covers it,' said the clerk emphatically.

I forgot all about her story until one day I found myself in the same situation, this time at our own Town Hall. The clerk was obviously a career woman, poised, efficient and possessed of a high-sounding title like, 'Official Interrogator' or 'Town Registrar'.

'What is your occupation?' she probed.

What made me say it? I do not know. The words simply popped out. 'I'm a Research Associate in the field of Child Development and Human Relations.'

The clerk paused, ball-point pen frozen in mid-air and looked up as though she had not heard right. I repeated the title slowly emphasising the most significant words.

Then I stared with wonder as my pronouncement was written in bold, black ink on the official questionnaire.

'Might I ask,' said the clerk with new interest, 'just what you do in your field?'

Coolly, without any trace of fluster in my voice, I heard myself reply, 'I have a continuing programme of research (what mother doesn't) in the laboratory and in the field (normally I would have said indoors and out).

'I'm working for my Masters (the whole darned family), and already have four credits (all daughters). Of course, the job is one of the most demanding in the humanities (any mother care to disagree?), and I often work 14 hours a day (24 is more like it). But the job is more challenging than most run-of-the-mill careers and the rewards are more of a satisfaction rather than just money.'

There was an increasing note of respect in the clerk's

voice as she completed the form, stood up and personally ushered me to the door.

As I drove into our driveway, buoyed up by my glamorous new career, I was greeted by my lab assistants – ages 13, 7 and 3. Upstairs I could hear our new experimental model (a six-month-old baby) in the child development programme, testing out a new vocal pattern.

I felt I had scored a beat on bureaucracy! And I had gone on the official records as someone more distinguished and indispensable to mankind than 'just another Mom'.

# Poetic Justice?

It doesn't have to be a premeditated act of revenge for the perpetrator to get even – intentionally or otherwise.

## Cat Got your Toe?

Cats are never grateful but this is taking things too far!

A 41-year-old German man was slicing bread when the knife slipped from his hand and fell to the floor – on to his bare foot, chopping off his second toe.

Udo Reid then hopped to the bathroom to get a bandage and to call the emergency services but while doing so, his cat Fritz seized the bloody toe and ran into the garden with his prize.

Reid tried to retrieve his toe from his cat but without success and he had to leave the cat with its 'tasty treat' to seek medical attention.

To rub salt in the wound, so to speak, the hospital staff confirmed that they would have been able to reattach the toe if Fritz had not run off with it.

## Gun Dog

When Bulgarian hunter Vasil Plovdiv's German Pointer dog refused to drop the quail it had retrieved, Vasil tried to dislodge the bird from his mouth using the butt of his rifle.

Not amused, the dog sprang at him, knocking the trigger and peppering the hunter's chest with shot.

# You're not singing any more!

It was the late, great Frank Sinatra who said, 'The best revenge is massive success' – a guiding principle by which he lived his life and managed his career. He spoke from experience having enjoyed early success in his twenties and early thirties before his career faltered. He then experienced about a decade with very little work. Fans and so-called friends deserted him. Against all the odds, in the 1950s, he secured some dramatic film roles that got his career back on track and Sinatra ended up as one of the most highly acclaimed male popular song vocalists of all time – massive success indeed.

There is another old saying, 'Be nice to people on your way up because you meet them on your way down,' originally coined by the American actor, comedian and pianist, Jimmy Durante. Perhaps some of those involved in the stories in this chapter should have borne this idiom in mind.

><  ><  ><  ><  ><  ><  ><  ><  ><

# That'll Show 'Em

When you are in the thick of a desperate situation and life seems pretty bleak, the old saying 'every cloud has a silver lining' purely serves to irritate rather than buoy the spirits. Yet, it's true that there are occasions when something good can come out of the worst scenarios, giving hapless individuals a lovely and probably unexpected last laugh, also known as sweet revenge, as the following stories show.

## Successful Writer

After her divorce, American author Sue Grafton wrote a crime thriller, *A Is For Alibi*, based on her vengeful thoughts about bumping off her ex-husband. Amazingly, despite the fact that she had never written before, the book took off and was the first in a chain of 19 alphabetical novels featuring private eye, Kinsey Millhone. Now on *S Is For Silence*, the novels have gained a cult following and Hollywood interest – and all because she dreamt of revenge on her ex-husband.

## Never Give Up

Roman Polanski, the acclaimed Polish film director, has had many highs and lows in his personal life and in his career ranging from the very worst moments, namely his mother dying in a World War II Nazi concentration camp and his heavily pregnant wife, Sharon Tate, being murdered, to sublime moments such as when he received his first best director Oscar for the movie *The Pianist* in 2002.

But he says of his low episodes, 'Every failure made me more confident. Because I wanted even more to achieve as revenge. To show that I could.'

## Famous Last Words

When photographer Michael Ward's great-grandfather, Theo, lay dying, word spread and the family gathered around his bedside. His seven children watched as he slowly slipped away. With one last effort, the patriarch leant forward, beckoning them to come closer:

'Can you all keep a secret?' he whispered.

They waited in anticipation for their father to divulge important news but, after a long silence, he said, 'So can I,' and died.

# Who's Laughing Now

We're reaching the end of our odyssey of revenge and it seems only fitting that we should finish on a high note, with the taste of sweet revenge in our mouths.

So let's celebrate the following selection of names who not only turned the tables but had the last laugh too. If only this bunch of critics could have known that massive success lay around the corner for the people they so cruelly dismissed. Who's laughing now, is what I'd say. Perhaps these detractors should have had a bit more faith … and a better eye for talent!

- ✂ 'It doesn't matter what he does, he will never amount to anything.' *Albert Einstein's teacher to his father in 1895.*
- ✂ 'We don't need you. You haven't got through college yet.' *Hewlett-Packard's rejection of Steve Jobs, who went on to found Apple Computers.*
- ✂ 'Balding, skinny, can dance a little,' *is how they summed up Fred Astaire at his first audition.*

# Revenge is Sweet

- ✂ '*Gone With the Wind* is going to be the biggest flop in Hollywood history. I'm just glad it'll be Clark Gable who's falling flat on his face and not Gary Cooper.' *Gary Cooper (after he turned down the role of Rhett Butler).*

- ✂ *Margaret Mitchell's novel* Gone with the Wind *was turned down thirty-eight times by publishers.*

- ✂ *H B Warner of Warner Brothers fame scoffed at the notion of 'talkies'. No one would want to hear movie actors talk, apparently.*

- ✂ *Walt Disney was fired for 'lacking ideas'.*

- ✂ 'He has no voice at all,' *said the teacher of Enrico Caruso — one of the world's greatest opera singers.*

- ✂ *Labelled as too awkward and clumsy to be a ball boy in a Davis Cup tennis match, Stan Smith went on to become the officially ranked number one tennis player in the world (1972–1973).*

- ✂ 'With over 50 foreign cars already on sale here, the Japanese auto industry isn't likely to carve out a big slice of the US market.' *Business Week, 1958*

- ✂ *As a would-be crime novelist, John Creasey received an unbroken succession of 743 rejection slips. Over 60 million of his books have now been published.*

- ✂ *A music teacher described his student as 'hopeless' at composing — the boy in question was Ludwig von Beethoven.*

✂ 'I think I may say without contradiction that when the Paris Exhibition closes, electric light will close with it, and no more will be heard of it.' *Professor Erasmus Wilson of Oxford University.*

# The Last Laugh

'I told you I was ill.'
*These words are on the gravestone of comic genius Spike Milligan.*

## Vanilla Pudding Robbery

Once inside the bank, shortly after midnight, their efforts at disabling the security system got underway immediately. The robbers, who expected to find one or two large safes filled with cash and valuables, were surprised to see hundreds of smaller safes throughout the bank.

The robbers cracked the first safe's combination, and inside they found only a small bowl of vanilla pudding. As recorded on the bank's audiotape system, one robber said, 'At least we'll have a bit to eat.'

The robbers opened up a second safe, and it also contained nothing but vanilla pudding. The process continued until all safes were opened. They did not find one pound sterling, a diamond, or an ounce of gold. Instead, all the safes contained covered bowls of pudding.

Disappointed, the robbers made a quiet exit, each leaving with nothing more than a queasy, uncomfortably full stomach.

The newspaper headline read: 'Ireland's Largest Sperm Bank Robbed Early This Morning'.

## What's Up, Doc?

A beautiful, voluptuous woman went to a gynaecologist. The doctor took one look at her, and all his professionalism went out the window.

He immediately told her to undress. After she had disrobed, the doctor began to stroke her thigh.

Doing so, he asked her, 'Do you know what I'm doing?'

'Yes,' she replied, 'you're checking for any abrasions or dermatological abnormalities.'

'That is right,' said the doctor.

He then began to fondle her breasts. 'Do you know what I'm doing now?'

'Yes,' the woman said, 'you're checking for any lumps or breast cancer.'

'Correct,' replied the shady doctor.

Finally, he mounted his patient and started having sexual intercourse with her. He asked, 'Do you know what I'm doing now?'

'Yes,' she said. 'You're getting herpes, which is why I came here in the first place.'

# References

**Papers and Surveys**

'Elephant Breakdown' by Joyce Poole *et al*, *Nature*, vol 433, p 801

'The Psychology of Workplace Revenge', by Dr Joni Johnston,www.workrelationships.com/site/articles/workplace_revenge.htm

The Computer Security Institute/FBI 2003 Computer Crime and Security Survey, *CSI Computer Security Institute*, vol 8, 2003

US Department of Justice, Cyber Crime Reports, www.cybercrime.gov/cccases.html

A 2004 Pokemon Institute Survey on Law Firm Security, *Ventura County Bar Association magazine*, www.vcba.org/citationsmag/2006/06may.pdf

Novell Survey on Disgruntled Employees (2003), *Connection Magazine*, www.novell.com/connectionmagazine/2006/q1/tech_talk_1.html

## Books

*Double Cross* by Sam and Chuck Giancana, Warner Books, 1993

*Fried Green Tomatoes at the Whistle Stop Café* by Fannie Flagg, Random House, 1997

*Gazza: My Story* by Paul Gascoigne, Headline Book Publishing, 2005

*Life's Little Annoyances: True Tales of People Who Just Can't Take It Anymore* by Ian Urbina, Times Books, 2005

## Published Studies and Pilot Studies

Al-Atoum, A O (1995) 'The Group Polarization Phenomenon: Can Group Discussion Lead to Polarization Decision Making', Dirasat, 22A(6), pp 2909–27

Baumeister, R F (2001) 'Social Psychology and Human Sexuality', www.psypress.co.uk

Bem (1981) 'Gender Schema Theory: A Cognitive Account of Sex Typing', *Psychological Review*, vol 88, pp 354–64

Bem (1981) *Bem Sex Role Inventory Professional Manual*, Consulting Psychologists Press

Crombag, H, *et al* (2003) 'Revenge Does Not Make Wounds Heal Faster: A Study at Universiteit Maastricht', *Research Magazine*, 9 October, www.unimaas.nl/researchmagazine/default.asp?id=65&thema=3&template=thema.html &taal=en

Forbes G B, *et al* (2005) 'Perceptions of Dating Violence Following a Sexual or Nonsexual Betrayal of Trust:

# References

Effects of Gender, Sexism, Acceptance of Rape Myths, and Vengeance Motivation', www.garfield.library.upenn.edu

Isozaki, M (1984) 'The Effect of Discussion on Polarization of Judgments', *Japanese Psychological Research*, vol 26, pp 187–93

Maccoun, R J and Kerr N L (1988) 'Asymmetrical Influence in Mock Jury Deliberations: Jurors' Bias for Leniency', *Journal of Personality and Social Psychology*, vol 54

Moscovici, S and Zavalloni, M (1969) 'The Group as a Polarizer of Attitudes', *Journal of Personality and Social Psychology*, vol 12, pp 125–35

Nairn, S L, *et al* (2006) 'The Cycle of Revenge: Gender, Response Severity, Group Discussion and the Social Acceptability of Retaliation', symposium presentation at the 2006 International Conference on Personal Relationships, Crete, Greece.

Schnake, *et al* (1997) 'Measure for Measure? Male Retaliation Commensurate with Anger Depends on Provocateur Gender and Aggression Covertness', *Journal of Social Behavior and Personality*, vol 12, pp 937–54

Sells, J N and Hargrave, T D (1998). 'Forgiveness: A Review of The Theoretical and Empirical Literature', *Journal of Family Therapy*, vol 20, pp 21–36

Singer T, *et al* (2006) 'Empathic Neural Responses are Modulated by the Perceived Fairness of Others', *Nature* Advanced Online Publication, 18 January, www.nature.com/nature/journal/v439/n7075/full/nature04271.html

Tripp, Thomas M, *et al* (2002) 'Aesthetics of Revenge: Poetic Justice or Petty Jealousy?', *Organizational Behavior and Human Decision Processes*, vol 89, no 1, September, pp 966–84, www.ingentaconnect.com/content/ap/ob ;jsessionid=npjrsdswsf7s.henrietta

## Websites

www.ananova.com
www.bbc.co.uk
www.breakupgirl.com
www.cats.about.com
www.dontdatehimgirl.com
www.lifeslittleannoyances.com
www.news.com.au
www.ratemyteacher.com
www.shameit.com.
www.SI.com
www.snopes.com
www.soufoaklin.com
www.urbanjunkies.com
www.walmartsucks.org

# Acknowledgements

I would like to thank all those brave souls who have contributed stories to this book and the many experts and professionals who have contributed. I would also like to acknowledge the great help and support of my friend and agent Chelsey Fox and my family.

Finally, if there's anyone I've missed who feels aggrieved, please don't resort to revenge!

# About the Author

Claire Gillman is a journalist, writer and broadcaster. She contributes to many leading women's magazines and writes on health, travel and parenting for national newspapers, including *The Times*. In the past, she was the editor of a number of consumer and specialist women's magazine titles including *Health & Fitness* and *Girl About Town*.

Claire's first book, *PARA: Inside The Parachute Regiment*, was published by Bloomsbury in May 1993. Since then she has published a further four adult health and parenting titles, and her book on the emotional aspects of dealing with ageing parents, *You and Your Ageing Parents: How to Balance Their Needs and Yours*, was published by Hodder & Stoughton in September 2005. In addition, she has written six children's books under the pen name of Rory Storm.

She is married with two adolescent sons and lives on the edge of the West Pennines with her family.